Senate Budget Committee
Library

CIVIL-
MILITARY
RELATIONS

CIVIL-MILITARY RELATIONS

Andrew J. Goodpaster
Samuel P. Huntington

In association with
Gene A. Sherrill and Orville Menard

With an introduction by Herbert Garfinkel

American Enterprise Institute for Public Policy Research
Washington, D.C.

Library of Congress Cataloging in Publication Data

Goodpaster, Andrew Jackson, 1915-
　　Civil-military relations.

　　(AEI studies ; 141)
　　Based on a Bicentennial symposium sponsored by the
University of Nebraska at Omaha and the American Enterprise
Institute for Public Policy Research.
　　Includes bibliographical references.
　　1. United States—Military policy.　2. United
States—Armed Forces.　3. Sociology, Military.
I. Huntington, Samuel P., joint author.　II. University
of Nebraska at Omaha.　III. American Enterprise Institute
for Public Policy Research.　IV. Title.
V. Series: American Enterprise Institute for Public
Policy Research. AEI studies ; 141.
UA23.G74　　　　322'.5　　　　77-960
ISBN 0-8447-3238-9

AEI studies 141

© 1977 by American Enterprise Institute for Public Policy Research,
Washington, D.C. Permission to quote from or to reproduce materials
in this publication is granted when due acknowledgment is made.

Printed in the United States of America

CONTENTS

INTRODUCTION *Herbert Garfinkel* — 1

1 THE SOLDIER AND THE STATE IN THE 1970s
Samuel P. Huntington — 5

The Problem of the Soldier and the State 5
Military Institutions and Liberal Society:
  The Historical Patterns 8
Constraints on the Level of Military Force 13
Constraints on the Use of Military Force 17
The Military and Society: Congruence and
  Interaction 22
Conclusion: The Dilemma Revisited 26

2 EDUCATIONAL ASPECTS OF CIVIL-MILITARY RELATIONS
Andrew J. Goodpaster — 29

Civil-Military Relations and Relationships 31
Educational Implications and Needs 34
Major Educational Programs 48
Broad Issues Ahead 53

3 A CASE STUDY OF CIVIL-MILITARY RELATIONS: ETHIOPIA
Gene A. Sherrill — 55

Historical View 55
Organizational Factors 66
Environmental Factors 70
Summary 74

4 REMARKS ON "EDUCATIONAL ASPECTS OF CIVIL-MILITARY RELATIONS" *Orville D. Menard*   **77**

    Public Opinion and the Military   77
    The Dangers of an Alienated Army   80
    The Role of Education   82

INTRODUCTION

Herbert Garfinkel

In most places and in most times, succession crises have been attended by the question, "What will the colonels do?" It was relevant in Argentina recently, and one can predict with confidence that it will crop up again as new coups d'état take place. On the other hand, when our own country was caught up in an extraordinary national crisis two years ago, when the constitutional commander-in-chief of the armed forces was besieged by his political opponents and the mass media were venting the full force of their reportorial sound and fury, no one seemed to be wondering about "the colonels."

Watergate was a test of the great constitutional principle of civilian control over the military—the fundamental law of civil-military relations under the American form of government. Perhaps we paid that principle our highest compliment by our seeming indifference to its existence. It is so firmly established, so fundamentally the basis of legitimate civil-military relations in the United States, that it went unnoticed precisely when put to the test.

The primacy of the principle of civilian control has a long history in our country. One of the charges leveled against King George by the American rebels in the Declaration of Independence was: "He has affected to render the military independent of and superior to the civil power." The legitimate balance between civil and military powers had been destroyed. In creating a new government, the framers of the Constitution sought "to provide for the common defense" in a way that would restore and guarantee that proper balance. Its stability in the face of Watergate is a measure of their success. Yet our vigilance, our informed sensitivity not just to the principle of civilian control, but also to the complexities of the relationship between the civilian and military sectors, are necessary to preserve it.

For the relationship can be skewed in two directions. Over the years, there has been a great deal of talk about the so-called military mind, and the stereotype contains more than a germ of truth: the domineering, rigid martinet is a fact of military history. Nor has the type been, unfortunately, without American examples. But the martinet bears the same relation to the truly professional military leader as the rigid bureaucrat bears to the truly professional administrator or the mere pedant to the scholar. To despise the military is to open the way for an oppressive form of civilian supremacy that would ultimately endanger our democratic values by leaving the nation effectively defenseless.

This volume is based on a symposium sponsored by the University of Nebraska at Omaha and the American Enterprise Institute for Public Policy Research and held at the Omaha campus in April 1976. On the occasion of the twenty-fifth anniversary of the Bootstrap program, which originated at the Omaha campus in 1950–51 and has permitted more than 11,000 military personnel to earn college degrees, the symposium brought together a distinguished soldier and a prominent scholar to discuss civil-military relations.

Samuel P. Huntington, professor of government at Harvard University, was asked to consider the validity of the argument advanced in his seminal work *The Soldier and the State* in the light of the events of the two decades since that work was published. In tracing the shifting patterns of civil-military relations in the United States, Huntington introduces a number of analytical concepts that illuminate the relationship between the military and society. The changes in attitudes toward the military that have taken place since the cold war and the persistence of the security threats that characterized that period, he concludes, leave us with an unresolved dilemma. As we seek to resolve it, Huntington believes, we must maintain the essential differences between the military and the society it serves, while minimizing the distance between them.

Education is one means of minimizing that distance, not only by promoting mutual understanding of the functions and problems of both sectors, but also by bringing military and civilian men and institutions together in joint educational programs. These and other educational aspects of civil-military relations are discussed in the symposium paper of General Andrew J. Goodpaster, former supreme allied commander in Europe. The comments on Goodpaster's paper by symposium panelist Orville Menard, professor of political science at the University of Nebraska at Omaha, highlight the conditions propitious for military intervention in the political sphere and the role of education in cultivating among both military men and civilians the civil values and traditions that can prevent those circumstances from arising.

Finally, Lieutenant Colonel Gene A. Sherrill, a participant in the Bootstrap program at the Omaha campus, has contributed a case study. His subject is Ethiopia, where the pressures of modernization in a backward, traditional society, long channelled for his own purposes by Emperor Haile Selassie, erupted in the form of a military coup in 1974. Sherrill's analysis of recent Ethiopian history illustrates the importance of many of the themes touched on in general terms by Goodpaster, Huntington, and Menard—the values held by the military, the nature and extent of military professionalism, the interaction of military and civilian elites.

Together these papers provide the basis for a continuing discussion of civil-military relations in the United States. The more seriously we pursue that discussion, the better equipped we will be to maintain enlightened civilian control of a strong and responsive military arm.

I wish to thank all those who participated in the symposium on civil-military relations, especially the following discussants of the two papers: Major General Andrew Anderson, Strategic Air Command chief of staff; Mr. Kermit Hansen, chairman of the board, U.S. National Bank, and member of the University of Nebraska Board of Regents; Brigadier General Phillip Kaplan, deputy director of military personnel management of the army; Dr. Orville Menard, professor of political science at the University of Nebraska at Omaha; Mr. Howard Silber, military affairs editor, *Omaha World Herald;* and Dr. A. Stanley Trickett, retired professor of history at the University of Nebraska at Omaha.

1
THE SOLDIER AND THE STATE IN THE 1970s

Samuel P. Huntington

The Problem of the Soldier and the State

"The military institutions of any society," in the opening words of *The Soldier and the State*,

> are shaped by two forces: a functional imperative stemming from the threats to the society's security and a societal imperative arising from the social forces, ideologies, and institutions dominant within the society. Military institutions which reflect only social values may be incapable of performing effectively their military function. On the other hand, it may be impossible to contain within society military institutions shaped purely by functional imperatives. The interaction of these two forces is the nub of the problem of civil-military relations.[1]

The military institutions of most societies embody a changing pattern of balance and accommodation between the societal imperatives and the functional ones. There is, however, no guarantee that the societal and functional imperatives will be reconcilable. Indeed, they sometimes clash head-on in such a way that one or the other has to give. Why should the patterns of political and technological development happily spare any particular society this unhappy choice? Why should other states frame their challenges to a particular society so that the society can meet those challenges in ways that are compatible with its basic political values and not discomforting to its ruling classes? Faced with certain threats, some societies may be

---

[1] Samuel P. Huntington, *The Soldier and the State: The Theory and Politics of Civil-Military Relations* (Cambridge, Mass.: Harvard University Press, 1957), p. 2.

incapable of providing for their own security except at the price of becoming something different from what they are.

The interaction between societal and functional imperatives manifests itself in a variety of ways. Of central importance, however, is the relationship between the military officer corps and the political institutions and leadership. The emergence of modern, developed societies has transformed the historical problem of civil-military relations. In less highly institutionalized and differentiated societies, the problem of civil-military relations centers on the twin issues of *military intervention* in politics through coups d'état and insurrections and of *military rule* of the polity, once the military have seized power and decide to keep it. In modern, developed societies, these are seldom the major problems. Such societies are characterized by relatively highly institutionalized political structures and patterns of rule (of which the Communist variant and the liberal democratic variant are the principal examples in today's world) and by relatively highly institutionalized and professionalized officer corps. The central problem of civil-military relations thus becomes the relationship between the military professionals and the political leadership.

In theory, this problem is not dissimilar from the broader issue of the relations between the generalist and the specialist, the politician and the expert. In the case of the military, however, it is often particularly intense and of central political importance to the society because of the nature of the functional imperatives that the military professional represents and because a highly professionalized and bureaucratized military establishment is, by its very nature, a potential source of political power and influence.

The modern officer corps is a highly professional body. It has its own expertise, corporateness, and responsibility. The existence of this profession tends to imply, and the practice of the profession tends to engender among its members, a distinctive outlook on international politics, the role of the state, the place of force and violence in human affairs, the nature of man and society, and the relationship of the military profession to the state. This professional military ethic tends to be one of conservative realism. Clearly, not all military officers adhere uniformly to it; indeed, in any military establishment very few officers possess the professional "military mind" in toto. It is instead an ideal type in the Weberian sense, and the interesting questions concern precisely why, how, and to what extent officers in different societies at different times deviate from this ideal type.

The ability of the officer corps to develop and maintain high standards of military professionalism and to adhere to the conservative realism of the military ethic depends upon the nature of the society it serves. If the values and ideology predominant in the society differ sharply from the conservative realism of the military ethic, the officer corps can acquire power in the society only by altering its attitudes and outlook to correspond more closely with those of the society. A totalitarian system cannot tolerate a military institution that controls substantial power but does not adhere to the political ideology of the regime. Civil-military relations in such regimes are almost always in a state of latent or actual crisis, as the all-encompassing demands of the state interact with the professional imperatives of the officer corps for autonomy. Political commissars, secret police, periodic purges, ideological indoctrination are the result: political control of the military, like political control of everything else, tends to be exerted in its most extreme form in the totalitarian state, whether Fascist or Communist.

The conservative realism of the professional military ethic also contrasts dramatically with the Lockeian liberalism that has predominated in American society. In large degree, there has been an American consensus and it has been a liberal, antimilitary consensus. Military forces, particularly professional military forces, and military institutions have been viewed with suspicion and hostility. The ideals of liberty, democracy, equality, and peace have contrasted with the military's concern with authority, hierarchy, obedience, force, and war. In theory and in practice, this fundamental ideological conflict can be resolved in one or more of three ways:

(1) The political power and functional importance of the military can be reduced so that the military exists as a conservative institution on the periphery of a liberal society, a policy of *extirpation*;

(2) The values and outlook of the military can change from conservative to liberal, thereby bringing the military into congruence with the society, and military functions can be broadened to include normally civilian ones, a policy of *transmutation*;

(3) The prevailing societal values can shift away from traditional liberalism in the direction of conservatism, society thereby adopting a policy of *toleration* with respect to the military.

These are the three theoretical options for accommodation between military institutions and a liberal society. At one time or another each has played a role in the American experience.

Military Institutions and Liberal Society: The Historical Patterns

Phase I: The Traditional Pattern. For the bulk of our history between 1815 and 1940 major threats to American security were few and remote. National security was a product of geographical location and of European politics, over neither of which the United States could exercise much control. National security was, in a sense, the starting point of policy, the assumption upon which policy was based rather than its product. Unconsciously and without concern, a liberal society could pursue a policy that was predominantly one of extirpation but partly too one of transmutation. Each successive group that rose to a preeminent role in American society had its own reasons for being suspicious of the military: to the eighteenth-century Whigs and Jeffersonians large military forces were a threat to liberty; the Jacksonians saw them as a threat to democracy; the dominant industrial and business groups after the Civil War saw them as a threat to economic productivity and prosperity; and the progressives and liberals saw them as a threat to reform. Almost everyone thought large standing military forces were a threat to peace.

The instrumental roles of the military forces were limited and relatively unimportant. In peacetime, these were, in the nineteenth century, largely confined to the pacification of the Indians and the protection of commerce from exotic pirates. In the twentieth century, the navy and Marine Corps were also used for various small-scale interventions in the Caribbean and Central America. The military forces maintained in peacetime were, in wartime, supplemented and largely overwhelmed and supplanted by militia units, reserve organizations, and other nonprofessional forces. Until World War I, even the major commands in wartime were in large part occupied by citizen-soldiers. The irrelevance of the standing forces in peacetime embodied the policy of extirpation; in wartime, their subordinate role reflected the ideals of transmutation: wars were too important to be fought by professional soldiers rather than by citizen soldiers. A sharp distinction was thought to exist between war and peace, and the role of regular military forces in either was limited.

As a result, the resources devoted to military purposes in peacetime were minimal throughout the nineteenth century and remained, by present-day standards, extraordinarily modest even after the beginning of the buildup of the navy early in the twentieth. An autonomous professional military officer corps did not emerge until the latter part of the nineteenth century, considerably later than in most major European countries. Before that time nonprofessional officers, of whom Jackson was the exemplar, often played leading political roles: this reflected the extent to which military functions were diffused through society. After the development of an autonomous profession, military officers faded from political roles outside the military establishment, which was itself too small to be a significant power base.

By and large, then, during Phase I the potential tensions between military institutions and liberal society remained latent because the lack of significant security threats made it possible to maintain, outside the mainstream of society, small military forces with little political influence, few economic resources, and marginal instrumental roles.

Phase II: The Cold War Pattern. After World War II, all of this, of course, changed drastically. National security suddenly became the overriding goal of policy rather than its starting point. Political elites and opinion makers saw the Soviet Union and the Communist bloc as posing major threats to that security, and the United States, they thought, must make substantial efforts to counter them. This produced five major changes in the traditional pattern of civil-military relations.

First, there was a tremendous qualitative and quantitative change in the instrumental roles of the armed forces. Military forces were necessary for nuclear deterrence, for deployment overseas in support of our allies in Western Europe and East Asia, and for rapid response to aggression and conflict in other parts of the world. Theories and policies were developed for deterrence, alliance management, and flexible response. Military force came to be viewed as a prime instrument of policy to prevent large-scale war and to deal with small-scale conflicts. Probably nothing is more striking in the contrast between the pre-World War II and post-World War II attitudes concerning civil-military relations than this change in attitude toward military force as an instrument of policy.

Second, the economic role of the military expanded tremendously. For twenty years beginning with the rearmament effort of the early 1950s—which brought into existence the military forces designed for the cold war—the military establishment commanded approximately 10 percent of the gross national product. A substantial armaments industry concentrated largely in aircraft, missiles, electronics, and shipbuilding came into existence to support the needs of that establishment.

Third, new governmental institutions were developed to organize and to control the military establishment, and significant changes took place in the roles of existing political institutions with respect to the military establishment. The National Security Acts of 1947 and 1949 legitimated the Joint Chiefs of Staff and created the Department of Defense, but they still left that department with one major deficiency, which was pointed out in *The Soldier and the State*. This was the relative weakness of the Office of the Secretary of Defense. The 1958 Defense Reorganization Act went a long way toward correcting this deficiency, and Secretary McNamara completed the task in the early 1960s with his vigorous administration of the office and his strengthening of its staff. With this, the organization of the department as a whole came close to achieving the "balanced" pattern that is most desirable for maximizing both civilian control and military effectiveness.

Coincidentally, significant changes took place in the roles of the President and Congress with respect to military policy. Prior to 1940, Congress did not hesitate to make strategic decisions on the weapons, force levels, and base systems of the armed forces. During the cold war, however, the primary locus of strategic "legislation" moved to the executive branch, with congressional groups at times playing significant roles as lobbyists and pleaders on behalf of one program or another, but not, by and large, exercising decision-making authority over such programs. Instead, the executive branch exercised that authority on force levels, weapons, deployments, and the use of force. Congress, however, continued to play its traditional role with respect to the "structural" side of the military establishment, that is, such issues as recruitment, pay, and other aspects of personnel policy, organization and administration, procurement policies and procedures, and issues connected with the reserve forces.

Fourth, the cold war period saw an end to the earlier isolation of the military establishment from other important segments of American society. In the immediate post-World War II years, large numbers of career officers moved into civilian roles in government and business. Subsequently, close relations developed between the military services and the business component of what was generally referred to as the military-industrial complex. Reliance on selective service for the procurement of enlisted men and the major role of the ROTC in officer procurement circulated through the armed services more-or-less representative samples of noncollege and college youth. The horizons of military education broadened, with the liberal arts and sciences playing a greater role in the curricula of the military academies and civilian lecturers and experts participating in greater numbers in the work of war colleges, staff colleges, and other military educational institutions. Even more important, large numbers of military officers were sent to civilian universities for advanced study in a variety of fields. Through Operation Bootstrap, more than 11,000 service personnel earned the bachelor of general studies degree in the twenty-five years after the program's inception in 1950–51. The military services, which had previously been isolated from American society, were now interacting vigorously with it.

Fifth, and perhaps most important because it was in a sense a precondition for these other changes, major shifts took place in the attitudes of the American public and elites toward the military services and military force. In effect, liberal antimilitary presuppositions and attitudes were at least temporarily weakened or suppressed, thus resolving in some measure the tension between military security and the liberal society. Some indications of this trend in the direction of a more conservative realism compatible with the professional military outlook were briefly sketched in the final chapter of *The Soldier and the State*. Indeed, the publication of *The Soldier and the State*, with its unabashed defense of the professional military ethic and rejection of traditional liberalism, was itself evidence of this changing intellectual climate. At the same time a large number of other books by scholars and journalists appeared that treated the military with a respect, and military needs with a consideration, most unusual in American history. The political and governmental elites of this period shared, by and large, an understanding and appreciation of the role of military force with respect to foreign policy matched only by that of the Federalists in the 1790s and the "Neo-Hamiltonians" in the 1890s.

These attitudes held by the intellectual and policy elites paralleled those that prevailed among the public. From the late 1940s until the mid-1960s, opinion surveys showed the mass public overwhelmingly opposed to reductions in U.S. military forces and budgets and a significant portion of the public in favor of increases in military strength. The Democratic majorities that dominated Congress through almost all of this period more often tried to increase spending for military programs than to reduce it significantly. On the use of force abroad, both public and Congress generally deferred to the President.

The Disruption of the Cold War Pattern. In the early 1970s, the cold war pattern of civil-military relations—a variant of the toleration option—clearly began to disintegrate as a result of the changes in the external and domestic environments that had made it possible in the first place. These changes may have been part of a broader antimilitary trend throughout the industrialized democracies as a result of higher levels of affluence and education, the decline of traditional authority, and changes in basic values. In addition, however, these changes had three distinct sources in the American experience.

First, the 1960s witnessed a momentous and dramatic change in the temper, scale, direction, intensity, and activity of American public life. This "democratic surge" involved the expansion of political participation, the introduction of new forms of participation, a significant polarization of opinion over social and foreign policy issues, the increased relevance of ideology to political behavior, and, most significant, a renewed commitment by various groups in American society to traditional American ideals of equality, liberty, democracy, and openness in government and a concomitant challenging of the authority of established political, economic, and social institutions. One key aspect of this surge was the redirection of public attention away from foreign affairs and concerns to the "neglected" priorities of domestic affairs: welfare, health, education, the environment, the cities. In somewhat paradoxical fashion, the surge thus produced both a major expansion of governmental activity (in domestic programs) and a major decrease in governmental authority.[2] This mobilization of opinion on behalf of reform had many similarities to the democratic surges that occurred in the Jacksonian and Progressive eras. The patterns of thought and behavior, the values that were articulated and the priorities that were set forth, had their precedents in these earlier periods. In the context of this reaffirmation of democratic and liberal values, continued adherence to the toleration option of the 1950s (which had involved the neglect or suppression of precisely those values) was no longer feasible.

A second major factor disrupting the cold war pattern of civil-military relations was, of course, the Vietnam War. Not only did this serve to galvanize and crystallize antimilitary sentiments latent beneath the surface of public opinion, but also it directly challenged the military's own perception of the proper balance in civil-military relations. It raised again in more acute and agonizing fashion the whole question of the limited use of military force for political purposes. This issue had, of course, come to the fore during the Korean War, but that case had simply involved the imposition by the political

---

[2] See the argument in my chapter on the United States in Michael Crozier, Samuel P. Huntington, Joji Watanuki, *The Crisis of Democracy* (New York: New York University Press, 1975), pp. 59 ff.

leadership of the government of restraints on how the military could fight a familiar type of war between sovereign states. In Vietnam, by contrast, the problems of guerrilla warfare, counterinsurgency, nation-building, and political development were central to the conflict, at least in its early phases. And these problems raised critical issues as to the role of military force in a civil war. In addition, the operation of the draft during the conflict brought into the military the "democratic surge" with its challenge to established authority, the counterculture, and the racial tensions then characteristic of American society. Instead of being tolerated by liberal society, the military establishment was now being invaded by it.

Third, changes in the international environment in the middle and late 1960s appeared to reduce the actual and potential external challenges to national security. On the one hand, there was the improvement in relations with both the Soviet Union and China, which seemed to decrease the probability of military conflict with either. On the other hand, there was a redefinition of American security interests; developments that had previously been conceived to be major threats were downgraded in terms of their implications for American security. Hence the impetus to maintain large, diverse, and extensively deployed military forces in the post-Vietnam era was considerably less than it had been previously. In the post-Vietnam, post-containment, post-cold war era of détente, what were large-scale military forces needed for? The Vietnam War became the only war in American history immediately after which military manpower levels and budget levels (in constant dollars) were significantly lower than they had been at the war's outset.

As a result of these three developments, civil-military relations in the 1970s entered a phase of confusion and flux. The brief cold war reign of the toleration option clearly is ending or being substantially modified. But what will take its place? A return to the traditional pattern? Some compromise between the traditional and cold war patterns? Some new arrangement differing from either of these historical models? In terms of maximizing military security at the least sacrifice of other social values, what pattern of civil-military relations should be developed?

Constraints on the Level of Military Force

"Previously the primary question was: what pattern of civil-military relations is most compatible with American liberal-democratic values? Now this has been supplanted by the more important issue: what pattern of civil-military relations will best maintain the security of the American nation?" This proposition in *The Soldier and the State* accurately reflected the prevailing attitudes and concerns of the 1950s. In the 1970s, however, as Douglas Rosenberg and Raoul Alcala accurately observe, "Huntington's statement appears curiously inverted today. Critics, scholars and policymakers have all begun to lose their preoccupation with external threats and to shift their attention to the effects of U.S. defense policy."[3] The 1970s, in short, witnessed a reversal of the reversal of the traditional liberal priorities that occurred in the 1950s.

This change in attitude was broadly visible across the board among elites, the attentive public, and the mass public. At the level of the mass public, opinion surveys showed a dramatic shift away from the permissive attitude toward military forces and even positive support for larger military forces that characterized the 1950s and early 1960s to widespread opposition. In the 1950s about 15 percent of the public wanted smaller military forces; in the early 1970s about 50 percent did. A Gallup poll for February 1957, typical of the era, revealed, for instance, that only 9 percent of the public favored a decrease in military spending, while 60 percent favored the existing level, and 22 percent favored an increase. In contrast, a poll taken in March 1971 showed that 50 percent of the public favored a decrease in military spending, 31 percent endorsed the existing level, and only 11 percent were in favor of an increase. "Recent antimilitary feeling," Bruce Russett wrote in 1974 in his summary of the poll data, "is absolutely unprecedented from the beginning of scientific opinion-sampling."[4] Opinion in Congress toward defense spending underwent comparable changes; in particular, the Democratic majorities of the 1950s, which had consistently attempted to increase military spending, were replaced in the 1970s by Democratic majorities that regularly attempted to reduce defense spending.

Widespread as it was, this change in attitude was, nonetheless, more marked among the elites and the attentive public than among the mass public. In the 1950s the "defense intellectuals" dominated

---

[3] Douglas H. Rosenberg and Raoul H. Alcala, "The New Politics of National Security: A Selected and Annotated Research Bibliography," in Bruce M. Russett and Alfred Stepan, eds., *Military Force and American Society* (New York: Harper & Row, 1973), p. 197.

[4] Bruce M. Russett, "The Revolt of the Masses: Public Opinion on Military Expenditures," in John P. Lovell and Philip S. Kronenberg, eds., *New Civil-Military Relations: The Agonies of Adjustment to Post-Vietnam Realities* (New Brunswick, N.J.: Transaction Books, 1974), p. 76.

the public debate of military matters. By the end of the 1960s, they had been superseded by a new corps of antidefense intellectuals, whose warnings of the dangers of militarism gave a very different tone to public discussion. "Antimilitarism," as Charles Moskos observed, "has become the anti-Semitism of the intellectual community."[5] The outpouring of antimilitary literature between 1968 and 1972 was, indeed, overwhelming. The old ideas of American liberalism in connection with military affairs came again to the surface. An overweening military establishment was a threat to peace, justice, liberty, the revisionists said. The attack on the military-industrial complex, on military institutions (such as the military academies), on military hierarchy and discipline, all sounded familiar themes that had been articulated many times before in American history.

Here we see another manifestation of the paradox of power in America. Ten years earlier, in 1961, President Eisenhower had spoken of some of the dangers inherent in the emergence of the military-industrial complex—whereupon the Kennedy administration had swept into power, dramatically increasing U.S. nuclear and conventional military strength. The power of the complex was, in a sense, reflected in the extent to which Eisenhower's warning was ignored. Ten years later, with military force-levels and budgets declining rather than rising, the intellectual elite became obsessed with the dangers of militarism. Their cries of warning about the power of the military, however, were testimony not to the extent of that power but rather to its waning. In American society, whenever the power of an organization or group is being exposed, it is also in the process of being reduced.

In the 1950s, the attitudes of the college-educated tended to be somewhat more promilitary than those of people with only grade-school education. In the 1970s, however, the roles were reversed: both groups were more antimilitary than they had been before, but the survey data show the college-educated group to be more antimilitary than those with grade-school education by about 15 percentage points. As Russett comments: *"antimilitarism is now strongest in the attentive public.* In other words, it is concentrated precisely in that part of the population most likely to vote, to express its opinions, to make campaign contributions and to participate in some form of organized political activity."[6] The antimilitarism of the late 1960s

---

[5] Charles C. Moskos, Jr., "Foreword," in Lovell and Kronenberg, *New Civil-Military Relationships*, p. xi.

[6] Russett in Lovell and Kronenberg, *New Civil-Military Relations*, p. 77. See also William Schneider, "Public Opinion: The Beginning of Ideology?" *Foreign Policy*,

and early 1970s reached an intensity unequalled since the 1920s and 1930s.

In 1975, however, the new wave of antimilitarism showed some signs of abating. The October 1973 Middle East War, the difficulties in negotiating SALT II, the collapse of South Vietnam, and the Soviet-Cuban intervention in Angola all modified somewhat the perceptions of the international environment that had prevailed five years earlier. In addition, the decline in democratic regimes in the less developed countries and the confrontations between developed and less developed countries over raw materials, trade, and the appropriate arrangements for the new international economic order all conjured up the image of a United States at odds with a hostile world. These factors, particularly when combined with a severe economic downturn, at least temporarily stilled the voices of antimilitarism, suspended congressional efforts to cut the military budget, and instead produced a general sympathy in Congress and the executive branch, among Democrats as well as Republicans, for modest increases in military spending. The idea that the military budget would increase gradually in real terms for the next several years became widely accepted.

Whether this recent turnabout in opinion is anything more than a temporary deviation from a more general trend remains uncertain at the present time. Antimilitary attitudes are particularly prevalent not only among the educated but also among the young. Consequently, it seems likely that they will have an influence on public policy for some while to come. On the other hand, the passion that characterized these attitudes during the Vietnam War has clearly abated. It thus seems possible that antimilitarism will become less fervent and more conventional, more like our traditional wisdom with respect to military matters, in which case a fair amount of discretion to determine the size and composition of the military forces will rest with political leaders. Just as antimilitarism is subsiding into indifference, so indifference may make way for a new toleration. But in the absence of a major international crisis, a return to anything resembling the cold war pattern of civil-military relations seems very unlikely.

Nevertheless, as long as antimilitarism is with us, particularly among the educated and the young, it will have two implications for the level of U.S. military forces. First, in the absence of a major international crisis, it will impose a real and important constraint

no. 17 (Winter 1974-75), p. 117: "The persistence of antimilitarism as an attitude associated with education represents a basic change in the traditional structure of foreign policy opinion."

on the level of those forces. Given the decline in the intensity, if not the scope, of antimilitary feeling, however, it seems likely that executive and congressional leaders will retain some freedom of action. Second, any significant reduction of this constraint will occur as the result either of a major international crisis or of actions taken by administration leaders to make it appear that a major international crisis exists. The latter course might well be adopted by an administration eager to reverse what it considered a long-term decline in relative U.S. military strength. The two major U.S. military buildups of the cold war years, indeed, were made politically possible by the accidental crisis of the Korean War and the largely manufactured crisis of the "missile gap." In the future, if administration leaders believe a military buildup is necessary to avert a crisis, they may have even greater incentives than did the leaders of the 1950s to create the appearance of a crisis in order to make that buildup acceptable to Congress and the public.

Constraints on the Use of Military Force

Until the 1950s the prevailing American view on the use of military force emphasized the distinction between war and peace. During peacetime, military force had little role to play except to furnish the base and the cadre for the mobilization of the forces that would be used in wartime. During war, on the other hand, military needs took precedence over all else; the policy was, in Woodrow Wilson's phrase, "force, force to the utmost," and the goal was total victory. The sharp distinction between diplomacy and war was appropriately symbolized by Secretary of State Hull's remark to Secretary of War Stimson, a few days before Pearl Harbor, concerning our deteriorating relations with Japan: "I have washed my hands of it, and it is now in the hands of you and Knox—the Army and the Navy." [7] During World War II, this view was, of course, reflected in the emphasis on unconditional surrender and the general unwillingness to consider the implications of the military conduct of the war for postwar politics and diplomacy. Diplomacy had no role in war, military force little or no role in peace.

During the 1950s, the Korean War, the conflict between General MacArthur and the government in Washington over the conduct of that war, and then Secretary of State Dulles's pronouncements on massive retaliation produced a remarkable change in the prevailing

---

[7] Quoted in *Soldier and State*, p. 317.

American attitudes on the use of force. The traditional dichotomy between war and peace, force and diplomacy, was replaced by a new stress on a continuum of conflict from war to peace and on the role of force as an instrument of policy and diplomacy. In effect, American strategists and policy makers came to think of military force in Clausewitzian terms: war is the instrument of politics, the continuation of politics by other means, and hence the use of force should not necessarily be "total" but instead limited to that necessary to achieve the political goals of the government. "The subordination of the military point of view to the political," is, therefore, as Clausewitz expressed it, "the only thing which is possible." The recognition by the defense intellectuals—of whom Bernard Brodie, William Kaufmann, Robert Osgood, and Henry Kissinger were most notable—and by others of the intimate relation between force and policy naturally led to the development of theories of limited war and graduated response. Since the government had to be prepared to exercise various military options across the spectrum of conflict, this also meant, of course, that the government had to maintain diverse and hence substantial military capabilities. The military buildup of the Kennedy years reflected, in large part, the impact of this doctrine.

The idea that force could be used for a variety of more or less important political purposes had implications for the constitutional and political processes by which the decisions on the use of force were made. Implicitly, the congressional power to declare war became equated with the power to declare total war. The commitment of forces to something less than total war was, in practice, done under the authority of the President, who acted with such consultation with Congress as he deemed appropriate.

The early 1970s saw a major reaction against this view of the relation of force to policy and against the related ideas of limited war, flexible response, and compellence as guides to the use of force. This reaction stemmed from many sources and manifested itself in many forms. It may well be the most portentous aspect of the disintegration of the cold war pattern of civil-military relations. It was expressed not so much in any decline in our military capabilities to engage in limited war but rather in political, legal, doctrinal, and psychological constraints upon our willingness to use those capabilities. Three of these constraints deserve particular attention.

First, there were some significant shifts in the willingness of mass public opinion to contemplate the use of force overseas. One 1974 poll, for instance, found that a majority of the American public with an opinion on the issue were opposed to the use of U.S. troops to defend Western Europe, West Berlin, or Yugoslavia against attack by the Soviet Union, Taiwan against attack by Communist China, South Korea against attack by North Korea, the Dominican Republic against attack by Cuba, or Israel against defeat by the Arabs. Interestingly, the relationship between elite and mass attitudes on the use of force tended to be the reverse of what it was on the level of force. Foreign policy elites were substantially in favor of the use of U.S. troops to defend Western Europe and West Berlin and were ambivalent about their use to protect the Dominican Republic and Israel. They were about as overwhelmingly opposed as the mass public to the use of U.S. forces to defend Taiwan, South Korea, or Yugoslavia. This hesitancy among both opinion leaders and the mass public concerning the use of U.S. forces overseas was, of course, one aspect of a much broader swing toward isolationism. In 1964, for instance, 8 percent of the American public could be classified as "total isolationists," while 65 percent were identified as "total internationalists." In 1974, the total isolationists had risen to 21 percent of the public, while the total internationalists had shrunk to 41 percent of the public.[8]

Public opinion surveys posing hypothetical questions and general questions are not necessarily a reliable guide as to what public opinion will be in the crunch or how it will respond to vigorous executive leadership. But public opinion does now constitute a potential constraint on the decision to use force that must be taken into account by policy makers. Beyond the question of the *initial* use of force by the government in response to conflict or aggression abroad, the Vietnam experience, when added to that of Korea, underlines the fact that public opinion clearly will not support the *sustained* use of force abroad. It is conceivable that if such sustained use were possible without recourse to conscription, it might be tolerated for a short while. There are, however, few contingencies that could involve the United States in combat for a sustained period of time without the government's resorting either to the draft or to a call-up of reserves, and even in contingencies where such measures were not necessary, public opinion would undoubtedly impose serious temporal limits on the use of U.S. forces.

---

[8] John E. Rielly, ed., *American Public Opinion and U.S. Foreign Policy 1975* (Chicago: Chicago Council on Foreign Relations, 1975), p. 18; *New York Times*, June 16, 1974, p. 3. For evidence of some shift in mass opinion in 1976 toward a greater willingness to aid in the defense of Western Europe and Japan, see William Watts and Lloyd A. Free, "Nationalism, Not Isolationism," *Foreign Policy*, no. 24 (Fall 1976), pp. 16-19.

Second, some indication of the nature of those temporal constraints is furnished by the legal limitations on the executive use of force contained in the War Powers Resolution of 1973. Under this act, the President must report promptly to Congress any introduction of U.S. forces into combat or any major new deployment of U.S. forces abroad. Such use of forces must then be terminated within sixty days unless Congress either declares war or specifically authorizes such use. When coupled with other legislation prohibiting the use of U.S. forces in Indochina (1973) and in Angola (1975), the likelihood seems small that Congress would authorize the sustained use of force under the War Powers Resolution for anything other than response to a major and direct challenge to vital U.S. security interests. Limited war on the model of the 1950s and 1960s has become a legal impossibility for the United States.

Third, the ideas of limited war and graduated response are being rejected on theoretical grounds. The Korean War inspired the doctrine of limited war; the Vietnam War did just the opposite. Vietnam is now being interpreted as a case in which the limited war theories of the 1950s were applied and found wanting. Flexible response and the gradual escalation of U.S. force did not produce the desired results. Instead, the prevailing argument now—advanced by both ex-hawks and ex-doves—is that a massive application of American power to North Vietnam in the early phases of the conflict might well have produced a relatively quick and satisfactory resolution of the conflict. Graduated response was, in General Westmoreland's words, "ill-considered," a "lamentable mistake," the product of "nebulous nonmilitary" considerations. The military judgment of the effects of the policy was well summed up by one air force officer: "We taught the bastards to cope." [9] And while the lessons drawn from Korea did not seem to work in Vietnam, the lessons drawn from Vietnam have been reapplied to Korea: "One of the lessons of the Vietnamese conflict," Secretary of Defense Schlesinger observed with Korea in mind, "is that rather than simply counter your opponent's thrusts, it is necessary to go to the heart of the opponent's power:

---

[9] Gen. William C. Westmoreland, *A Soldier Reports* (Garden City, N.Y.: Doubleday & Co., 1976), pp. 112, 119, 195-96, 410; Franklin D. Margiotta, "A Military Elite in Transition: Air Force Leaders in the 1980s," *Armed Forces and Society*, vol. 2 (Winter 1976), p. 162. For a definitive analysis of the views of the top military commanders and civilian advisors on the use of force during the cold war years, see Richard K. Betts, "Soldiers, Statesmen, and Resort to Force: American Military Influence in Crisis Decisions, 1945-1975" (Ph.D. thesis, Harvard University, 1975).

destroy his military forces rather than simply being involved endlessly in ancillary military operations."[10]

Thus, prevailing American opinion on the use of force appears to have reverted to the pre-World War II assumption of a sharp dichotomy between war and peace. In fact, there has been a marked decline in the past eight years in the peaceful use of force by the United States to support its diplomacy.[11] But is the separation of force and diplomacy a realistic and constructive assumption with which to confront the 1970s and the 1980s? At the end of the Korean War, the then secretary of defense, Charles E. Wilson, remarked, "I do not think we could fight another Korea and not use all the resources necessary to win the war. . . . I do not think the American people would be in favor of another one like that." Vietnam proved Wilson a good political prophet. On the other hand, Wilson's successor during the Vietnam War, Robert McNamara, had, at least for a while, a somewhat different view:

> The greatest contribution Vietnam is making—right or wrong is beside the point—is that it is developing an ability in the United States to fight a limited war, to go to war without the necessity of arousing the public ire. In that sense, Vietnam is almost a necessity in our history, because this is the kind of war we'll likely be facing for the next fifty years.[12]

McNamara could be right in his judgment about future military contingencies; Wilson could be right in his judgment about the constraints on how we can deal with these contingencies.

Political, legal, and military factors thus all lead to a rejection of what seemed to be the sophisticated doctrines of the 1950s on limited war and graduated response. The reaction of the doves against the way we got into the Vietnam War reinforces the reaction of the hawks against the way we fought it. A future Vietnam is more likely to last seven weeks than seven years. The United States will probably be slower to resort to force in the future than it has been in the past, but when it does, it will apply overwhelming force

---

[10] *U.S. News & World Report*, May 26, 1975, p. 25.

[11] Barry Blechman of the Brookings Institution has developed quantitative data demonstrating this decline.

[12] Quoted in Samuel P. Huntington, "Democracy Fights a Limited War: Korea, 1950-1953," in Merrill F. Peterson and Leonard W. Levy, eds., *Major Crises in American History: Documentary Problems* (New York: Harcourt, Brace and World, 1962), vol. 2, p. 481, and Douglas H. Rosenberg, "Arms and the American Way: The Ideological Dimension of Military Growth," in Russett and Stepan, *Military Force*, p. 170.

in order to achieve its objectives quickly and decisively. The emphasis will be on limiting the duration of the conflict, not on limiting the means. In this sense, future aggressors may well end up paying part of the cost of the failure of the U.S. military strategy in Vietnam.

The Military and Society: Congruence and Interaction

The changes in the environment of the military have also had an impact on the military establishment itself. They have raised the question whether the military establishment will continue to tend toward "civilianization" and convergence with social institutions or whether this trend has been reversed in the direction of remilitarization and a renewed stress on traditional military values and behavior. And beyond this, which tendency ought to be encouraged? Is convergence or insulation the more desirable course for the military establishment in the post-Vietnam world? Military officers, principally field grade officers, have engaged in a wide-ranging and most impressive discussion of these questions.

A useful analysis of these issues requires that a sharp distinction be made between two dimensions of the convergence-isolation dichotomy. On the one hand, there is the issue of the *congruence* between the military establishment and society or other social institutions, that is, the extent of their similarity or difference in terms of personnel, functions, structure, and other salient characteristics. Second, there is the issue of *interaction* between the military establishment and society or other social institutions, that is, the extent to which military institutions and individuals have a multiplicity of contacts with nonmilitary institutions and individuals.

The distinction between congruence and interaction is important because, as David Segal and his associates have usefully reminded us, there is quite possibly a tendency for levels of congruence to vary inversely with levels of interaction. A military establishment, they argue, that encompasses many nonmilitary functions and that operates in a civilianized manner is likely to be more autonomous—freer from civilian contacts and, potentially, civilian control—than a military establishment that is purely military and that, precisely because of its specialization, is dependent upon civilian society for support.[13] Clearly, there is a certain logic to this argument. On the other hand,

---

[13] David R. Segal et al., "Convergence, Isomorphism, and Interdependence at the Civil-Military Interface," *Journal of Political and Military Sociology*, vol. 2 (Fall 1974), pp. 157ff.

Table 2-1

ALTERNATIVE RELATIONS BETWEEN THE MILITARY AND SOCIETY

Level of Interaction	Level of Congruence	
	Low	High
Low	Insulation	Self-sufficiency
High	Professionalism	Identification

it is perhaps more useful to envision congruence and interaction as two separate dimensions of civil-military relations susceptible to a variety of possible combinations in both theory and practice (see Table 2-1). A self-sufficient military establishment would indeed be characterized by a high level of congruence and a low level of interaction. As Segal and his associates suggest, such a situation has been approximated by U.S. forces stationed abroad in their relations with the surrounding societies. On the other hand, a high level of congruence could also exist in a military establishment with a very high level of interaction, and even identification, with society; this is the pattern implied by the nation-in-arms concept and embodied in some measure in the practice of countries like Israel and Switzerland. Third, a military establishment with a low level of congruence with civilian society—that is, one highly specialized in its military functions— might also have a low level of interaction, as tended to be the case with the U.S. military establishment in the late nineteenth century. Finally, a professional relationship might be said to exist when there is a relatively low level of congruence, reflecting specialization, but a relatively high level of interaction, reflecting responsiveness to civilian society.

Recent trends in the U.S. military establishment have been in the direction of lower levels of congruence and, to a lesser degree, lower levels of interaction in relation to civilian society. During the cold war period, for instance, both the officers and the enlisted personnel of the armed forces were recruited from fairly diverse sources in civilian society. The shift to purely volunteer recruitment of enlisted personnel undoubtedly will make the enlisted personnel of the armed services less representative of the civilian population as a whole. How drastically the social composition of the military will be altered, however, at the moment remains unclear and is, indeed, a matter of considerable dispute. The expanded role of the military academies in providing officers is likely to raise the proportion of officers whose values and attitudes, if not necessarily their social origins, differ from those of civilian leadership groups. In addition, the increasing predominance among ROTC programs of those operated by smaller colleges and universities, particularly in the South and West, may reinforce a growing gap between military leaders and economic and political elites. As we noted above, the latter tend to have fairly strong latent if not active antimilitary attitudes. Thus, in terms of personnel, the level of congruence between the military and other social institutions appears to be declining.

With respect to functions, recent analyses have stressed the extent to which the trend toward convergence between the military occupational structure and the civilian occupational structures has ceased and perhaps even been reversed. In addition, as between military and civilian institutions, there seems to be "a reaffirmation, in the current decade, of a traditional division of labor that perhaps did get blurred in the early 1960s."[14] Or, as another observer put it, with the decline of the mass army, there is also a tendency toward "remilitarization" and an abandonment of the "school of the nation" functions that modern armies have sometimes assumed.[15] In military educational institutions, broad courses on international affairs have yielded to a stress on more "purely military" topics. At the same time, however, sharply differing views are held by analysts, both civilian and military, as to whether this or the reverse course is the more desirable. Some have argued for a wider concept of military professionalism, challenging the argument of *The Soldier and the State* that the essential task of the military is "the management of violence" and positing a much broader administrative and managerial role for professional military officers. Other officers have urged a reaffirmation of the traditional concept. Similar debates have gone on over the desirability of the armed forces' assuming responsibility for "domestic action" or "civic action" programs unrelated to their national security functions.[16] But while these debates have

---

[14] Ibid., p. 169.

[15] Jacques van Doorn, "The Decline of the Mass Army in the West: General Reflections," *Armed Forces and Society*, vol. 1 (Winter 1975), p. 155.

[16] For some of the views held by military officers on these issues, see Richard F. Rosser, "A Twentieth Century Military Force," *Foreign Policy*, no. 12 (Fall 1973), pp. 156ff.; Edwin A. Deagle, Jr., "Contemporary Professionalism and Future Military Leadership," *The Annals of the American Academy of Political and Social Science*, vol. 406 (March 1973), pp. 162ff.; Robert G. Gard, Jr., "The Future of the Military Profession," in *Force in Modern Societies: The Military Profes-*

been raging, the trends toward military role expansion and functional congruence between the military establishment and civilian institutions have shown signs of coming to a halt.

Finally, with respect to the structure of the military, strong tendencies existed in the late 1960s and early 1970s toward convergence with civilian patterns. Much of the civil turmoil, many of the changes in life style of those years, manifested themselves in the armed services as well as in civilian society. Traditional concepts of rank, discipline, and social relations were reexamined, and efforts were made—in the navy under Zumwalt, for example—to stress the similarities between life styles and human relations within the military establishment and those outside. One recruitment slogan read, "The Army wants to join you!" Some officers suggested even further alterations in the traditional military structure, such as abolition of the "two-caste" division between officers and enlisted men in favor of a single nondiscontinuous hierarchy.[17] At present, however, the trend toward structural congruence between military and civilian institutions, like the trend toward functional congruence, seems to have leveled off.

In general, then, the level of congruence in terms of personnel, function, and structure between the military establishment and civilian institutions seems to be declining. The evidence concerning patterns of interaction is more mixed, but here again the dominant trends appear to be downward. In the long run, voluntary recruitment will reduce the interaction between the military and society as well as having its impact on the level of congruence. Congressional efforts to reduce the numbers of military officers attending civilian institutions of higher education are further evidence of the decline of both interaction and congruence between military and civilian institutions. One proposal espoused by many army officers in the early 1970s was that the military itself be sharply divided into "com-

---

sion, Adelphi Paper No. 103 (London: International Institute of Strategic Studies, 1973), pp. 1-8; Zeb B. Bradford, Jr., and Frederic J. Brown, *The United States Army in Transition* (Beverly Hills: Sage Publications, 1974), chaps. 13, 14; William L. Hauser, *America's Army in Crisis: A Study in Civil-Military Relations* (Baltimore: Johns Hopkins University Press, 1973), chap. 12; William R. Corson, "Towards a Concept of Military Domestic Action" (Unpublished paper, Inter-University Seminar on Armed Forces and Society, September 1971).

[17] See, for example, Rosser, "Twentieth Century Military Force," and the ideas canvassed in *Rapporteur's Report: First Inter-Service Defense Policy Conference, 10-12 May 1972* (Department of Political Science, United States Air Force Academy and the National Security Program, Graduate School of Public Administration, New York University).

bat forces" and "support forces."[18] The former would, in most respects, be very noncongruent with civilian institutions and would have little interaction with the civilian sector. The various components of the support forces, on the other hand, would be very similar in operation and function to parallel civilian groups and would have significant interaction, including personnel interchanges, with those groups. The prospects for such a neat sorting out of these relationships seems remote. Indeed, if this proposal were implemented the problems of congruence and interaction between the military and society that now exist would merely be duplicated within the military in the relations between the combat forces and the support forces.

Conclusion: The Dilemma Revisited

The argument advanced in *The Soldier and the State* in 1957 was that, given the existing international situation, "the requisite for military security" was a shift from liberalism to a "sympathetically conservative" attitude toward the needs of military professionalism. To a surprising extent, that shift occurred. In some measure, also, it has now been reversed. The immediate future would thus appear to involve a combination of the liberal attitudes dominant before World War II (Phase I), but repressed during the cold war (Phase II) with the security threats nonexistent in Phase I but predominant in Phase II. The dilemma that was partially resolved in the 1950s has returned.

For the immediate future, civil-military relations in the United States will be characterized by loosely constraining public attitudes and more tightly constraining elite attitudes on military force levels. More important, both public and elite opinion will impose severe constraints on the future uses of our military forces. At the same time, although a variety of conflicting pressures will be at work, the prevailing trend will be toward less congruence and possibly less interaction between the military establishment and other social institutions. The toleration that characterized the cold war period of civil-military relations is not likely to be superseded by traditional extremes of either extirpation or transmutation. As the effects of the democratic surge, the Vietnam War, and the enthusiasm for détente fade into the past, the prevailing attitude of American society toward

---

[18] This was proposed by Charles C. Moskos, Jr., "The Emergent Military: Civil, Traditional or Plural," *Pacific Sociological Review*, vol. 16 (April 1973), pp. 255ff. Similar arguments are advanced in: Rosser, "Twentieth Century Military Force"; Hauser, *America's Army*; Bradford and Brown, *Army in Transition*.

its military forces is likely to be one of modified or contingent toleration. This attitude will be reinforced if the military limit the extent to which they turn inward and instead emphasize their professional military functions and characteristics without self-consciously breaking their ties with civilian society. In the end, the dilemma of military institutions in a liberal society can only be resolved satisfactorily by a military establishment that is *different from but not distant from* the society it serves.

2
EDUCATIONAL ASPECTS OF CIVIL-MILITARY RELATIONS

Andrew J. Goodpaster

Knowledge is power, in military as in other fields of human action. But if military power is to serve human needs well it must be controlled and restrained. Knowledge is needed to produce military power; it is also needed to control it, and education is essential to both purposes. In the dangerous world in which we live, where military power is an indispensable though expensive necessity for national safety and well-being, these considerations provide the basis for a careful examination of the educational aspects of civil-military relations.

Civil-military relations are often thought of in terms of the direction and control of military activity and military power already in being. But they go deeper. They are involved as well in the shaping of military power—the determination of its magnitude, composition, and readiness for employment.

The civil-military relations intrinsic to the creation, upkeep, and operation of military forces generate a multiplicity of educational needs and processes, if these relations themselves and the substantive activities to which they pertain are to be correctly understood and sensibly regulated. And the education itself, by which servicemen are assisted in preparing themselves to do their jobs effectively, in turn generates important and sensitive civil-military relations, especially between the military and the academic community.

To examine the educational aspects of civil-military relations, we must analyze in some detail several subtopics: civil-military relations and relationships, the military requirements and constraints that flow from such relationships, the educational implications and needs that

Note: Parts of this paper reflect research the author pursued as a fellow of the Woodrow Wilson International Center for Scholars during 1975 and 1976.

derive from these, the educational activities and programs that respond to these implications and needs, and the broad issues that arise in connection with these activities, together with the possible direction in which valid responses to these issues may be found. In this discussion, the educational aspects of civil-military relations will be viewed primarily from the standpoint of the military establishment. In the process, many of the principal considerations that are of interest from the standpoint of society as a whole will also be developed.

The title of this paper would permit us, on the one hand, to confine ourselves to a consideration of the teaching of the subject of civil-military relations in the traditional terms of civilian control, sources of civil-military stress and strain, and so on. Alternatively, it might be interpreted as calling for an examination on a broader canvas of the educational implications and needs that derive from the relation of military functions and institutions to the fundamental goals, values, processes, and institutions of our basically civilian society. It is the latter, wider scope of examination (which may of course provide substantive material for the teaching task) that has been adopted for this study.

Accordingly, it is worth stressing at the outset that all educational activities, needs, problems, and processes that involve our military institutions and their members fall within the confines of "civil-military" relations as herein delineated. This means that we are dealing with a highly diversified process, massive in its dimensions, far-reaching in its effects. In an aggregate military force of some 2 million, nearly 250,000 men and women are at any moment the recipients of individual training and education, and nearly the same number again are involved in the administration, direction, and support of this group.

The education and training that are received by military personnel are of many different kinds, administered at many different levels, and designed for many different purposes; they involve scores of categories of participants and serve the needs of a great variety of sponsors. Much of the education and training received by military men and women is conducted by the military itself, but much is conducted by civilian institutions. Some of it is conducted before the individuals enter the military service—the collegiate studies of officers-to-be enrolled in the ROTC, for example; but much is conducted during the term of military service. Most is undertaken for the benefit of the military establishment, to strengthen its management, operation, and organizational readiness; but a not inconsiderable amount is intended largely for the benefit of the individual, during his military service, afterwards, or both during and afterwards. Beyond the whole realm of individual training and education lies unit and organizational training, a tremendously vital part of the individual learning and institution-building process, essentially beyond the scope of the present discussion, though performed within the civil-military relationship that characterizes all military activity.

Civil-Military Relations and Relationships

To see civil-military relations in a true light, one must view them in the broadest possible context, the role of the military in our national society. The basic civil-military relationship is simply one of service: the military serves the parent civil society. The military establishment is designed, operated, and supported to serve goals and interests—in particular, security goals and interests—of the society at large. This is the fundamental, all-embracing relationship of civil and military in our democratically governed society, and all that the military is or does should be aligned to these goals. This relationship has not always or everywhere been the guide; in other countries, for example, both in the past and today, military and political power have often been consolidated, and where the two have been differentiated military power has often been supreme. The contrary tradition, which we enjoy, has shaped and guided our military forces since our government was founded and our national society was formed.

For national societies as for individuals, safety and self-preservation remain the first law of life. Today as in the past, the security interests of our people require that they, their territory, and their commerce be protected against attack and against outside pressures or efforts at coercion and interference based upon threats of military attack. A new factor in the thermonuclear age is the increasing stress that is properly placed upon accomplishing these objectives without actual conflict—that is, avoiding war while safeguarding national freedom, peace, safety, confidence, and well-being. Furthermore, these goals must be met in the present in a way that does not prejudice their continued fulfillment in the future, as far ahead as we can see. The imperatives of national security are increasingly complex and the stakes ever higher in an era when the certainty of mass destruction through reciprocal nuclear missile attacks lies less than one hour's flight time past a moment of final, irrevocable decision. This all-embracing security interest lies at the heart of the relationship between the military and the civil components of our society and defines the framework within which more detailed relations must be examined.

The aspect of civil-military relations to which attention is often first given is the tradition of civil control over military power. The principle itself is clear: under our system, the military does what the civil authority determines, and only that; it does not do otherwise. The application of this principle, however, is complex and difficult, for one fundamental reason: There is a vast, diverse, intricately interwoven body of military knowledge, expertise, procedure, and organization that is indispensable to effective and economical military results consonant with the values and ideals of our society. Their interpretation is not an area in which the amateur excels, not even the brilliant amateur. It is not that all wisdom resides in the military; far from it. Civilian students of strategy, operations procedures, intelligence methods, procurement practices, educational methods, and training techniques have offered much in the past and continue to do so, though such contributions, be it noted, have not come without effort or intensive application to the facts. But it is the test of combat, or the perceived probable results of the test of combat—the unique domain of the military professional—that ultimately and fundamentally establishes the validity of military posture and action.

A key task is to design and operate the links that tie this military expertise to the higher echelons of governmental decision and, beyond them, to the ultimate source of political power, values, and decisions, the people themselves. In part, the necessary control can be exercised by the provisions of law, by policy instructions and regulations, by consideration and approval of specific proposals, and by inspection, audit, and review of the performance of military establishments. In some areas, the practice has grown up of placing sizable civilian contingents within the defense structure itself—in the Pentagon, for example—particularly in functions such as manpower, facilities, procurement, telecommunications, research and development, and intelligence, which involve a considerable degree of contact with the members of the civilian community and with their congressional representatives. But there remains a need, particularly at the higher levels of military responsibility, for deep, well-informed understanding of these relationships on the part of the military leaders and their staffs. It should be recalled that the military leadership has the responsibility to inform and advise in the formulation of policies and the decision making at the national level by which they will then be guided. Theirs is not, however, a determining role. The National Security Act provides that the Joint Chiefs of Staff are the principal military advisors to the President, the National Security Council, and the secretary of defense.

The civil society is the source of the funds, resources, and manpower from which the military forces and their supporting establishment are built and sustained. The government—that is, the executive, through the formulation and management of the budget, and the Congress, through legislative authorization and appropriation—determines not only what resources will be made available for military purposes but also (and in tremendous detail) how they are to be structured into programs and forces in being. But the society itself has a further, more fundamental role beyond the validation or rejection of the actions of the government. The government cannot make available what does not exist. Military power cannot outpace what is reasonably susceptible of being made available. Ultimately, civilian society must decide the relative weight it wishes to give to defense and to opulence, in the famous phrase of Adam Smith. But military men at the higher levels of responsibility must have understanding of and respect for the processes by which the society and its government make such determinations.

The academic community is a particular segment of civil society as ultimate source of military strength that is of special interest to this discussion. Its involvement with military activities and issues will be traced in more detail later. Here we may note that the academic community is a major source of education for the individuals who compose the military establishment—directly, through the preservice and during-service education that such individuals receive from civilian institutions, and indirectly through the elaborate educational process internal to the military, manned by officers and enlisted personnel whose principal educational preparation was at civilian hands. (Even in military schools, furthermore, much of the pedagogic substance is the work of civilian authors, teachers, or researchers.)

Shaping the patterns of civil-military relations are the attitudes toward their military institutions held by the civil community. We well know that these attitudes are shifting, sometimes volatile. Of particular importance is the degree to which the society at large identifies with the military as an inherent specialized component essential to its own well-being—or regards it instead, in a kind of adversary relationship, as a competing, burdensome entity that endangers its sons and draws our country into distant and perilous adventures. Obviously, it is a mixture of the two attitudes that most often prevails, a mixture the dominant component of which varies from one sector of society to another.

The rise of resentment toward the American military during the Vietnam War, particularly sharp among the opinion-forming elite but later more widely reflected within the society at large and the Congress, is bound to have long-lasting effects. This resentment may prove to have characterized a single generation of American attitudes centering on the years 1965 to 1975, but it is also possible that the pronounced alienation between, on the one hand, the military and others concerned with national security and, on the other hand, much of the influential media and the academic community in particular will prove to be permanent, or at least long term. For the moment, the mood is unquestionably disinterested, negative, even hostile, though in some quarters the intensity of feelings seems to be lessening. As a new generation of students enters the colleges and universities, a generation not threatened by the draft, campus pressures have markedly declined. Attention and emotional involvement have shifted to a new range of domestic problems and away from military issues. This development in itself, however, is hardly reassuring to the military. Many of the new concerns—inflation, unemployment, budgetary stringency, impaired political leadership, the incapacity of government to solve salient economic and social problems, disillusionment at political misdeeds—tend to encourage mistrust of government and complacency toward military needs and dangers, and these attitudes, reflected in the Congress, can have a strongly adverse effect upon military programs and activities.

Finally, in America there is not and has never been a military caste. Our military establishment is drawn from all corners and all levels of society, in most cases educated through high school or college in the civilian community and due to return, after one or more terms of enlistment or of obligated service or after a military career, to the civilian community, some in retirement but many more in some other form of gainful employment.

There are, of course, a multitude of more specific ways in which the civil and military sectors interact, but these will perhaps suffice to suggest the principal elements of the role of the military vis-à-vis civil authority and the society at large.

Educational Implications and Needs

If our military establishment is to fulfill its assigned role and do so in ways acceptable to the parent society, it must meet demanding standards of performance. Extensive programs of precise, coordinated training and education in a wide range of studies are needed. Individual competences must be developed in many subject areas. The process must meet exacting criteria of effectiveness and economy and gain sustained support and acceptability by the public, by the participating colleges and universities, and by the Congress—especially the Armed Services and Appropriations committees.

The basis of the educational needs in and for the military is the pattern of military functions and responsibilities. These responsibilities involve command and leadership at every level—from an army company, a navy ship, or an air force air squadron up to a unified command such as the Strategic Air Command or the forces of the European Theater. Responsiveness to higher levels of authority and advice and recommendation to such higher levels are constantly required of military officers. At top levels, these functions require participation in the work of the National Security Council structure and close and cooperative contact with the State Department, the Arms Control and Disarmament Agency, the Central Intelligence Agency, the Energy Research and Development Administration (the former Atomic Energy Commission), and similar governmental agencies. The substance of the work ranges from management and budgeting, personnel, logistics, communication, and intelligence to operations, organization, plans, and policy.

In subjects that are uniquely or primarily military, the educational needs of military personnel are met in military schools. But many subjects in which military personnel require training lie in areas of educational need that the military shares with the civilian community, and programs in these subjects can best be civilian based.

Major changes are taking place in the patterns of military responsibilities that education must serve. Reduction in some of our foreign commitments, the emergence of new areas of crisis and danger, the introduction of new American and Soviet strategic missiles and aircraft, force consolidations and changes in deployment, computerization of logistics and administration—these and a flood of other changes subject our military activities to constant modification at every level. Old policies are being discarded, but what is to take their place is far from clear. Because educational lead times are so long, however, decisions must be made and programs shaped today to prepare for a future that is still uncertain. Fortunately, guideposts are not wholly lacking. The fundamental responsibilities of the military, of course, will not change, and these provide useful guidance as to future educational needs. They include national security interests; security policies such as defense, deterrence, and détente; the major combat tasks our military must be prepared to perform; and major programs and processes of force development. In a situation so much in flux, heightened awareness of these guideposts becomes essential.

National Security Interests. First among the considerations determining the role and educational needs of the military are the national security interests of the United States. These have a large component that retains its validity even in these turbulent times. It is still possible to identify with considerable assurance the major interests that we must recognize and pursue with respect to Russia and China, the Western-style industrialized democracies, and the diverse countries of the world beyond in order to provide the safety, freedom from outside interference, and friendly association with other countries that are essential to our national well-being. So long as the outward reach for domination over others by Communist regimes under the direction of Moscow and Peking continues, our interests may be endangered at many points; so long as the Communist powers hold in their hands such tremendous military power as they have today, it will be in our interest—an interest we cannot evade—to counterbalance and constrain them. In part, this requirement can be met by direct, unilateral means, that is, by mounting and maintaining similar forces of our own, U.S. air and missile forces and naval forces in particular. But in good part, it is necessary for us to concert our preparations with those of other nations, major allies joined with us in mutual security arrangements: the NATO countries in the Atlantic and European areas and Japan and Korea, at the very least, in Asia and the Pacific. Such arrangements, for the foreseeable future, will remain essential to the stability and confidence upon which world order and national well-being will largely depend. Here too, the military implications are clear, as are the educational needs that flow from them: understanding of our allies and of ways of working with them in highly developed multinational institutions such as those of NATO.

In the world beyond, the situation is less clear. Indeed, it is particularly obscure just at this moment, when the experiences of Vietnam and Angola show unmistakably what Congress will *not* allow in the way of making and supporting commitments, but when no definite guidelines have emerged as to what commitments Congress *will* allow. The absence of a consensus has left the United States, in effect, without a policy other than a de facto posture of inaction and disregard for the outcome of conflicts in distant places that do not directly or immediately affect U.S. national life. Thus far, there has been little interference with the free use of the high seas, but the

U.S. reaction to the Cambodian seizure of the *Mayaguez* in early 1975 provides some clue as to what the public attitude might be should such instances recur. Even this example is not free from ambiguity, however, since the action taken was of small scale, was completed swiftly, and did not await prior consideration by Congress.

Despite the uncertainties, it would be premature—and probably inconsistent with the more considered public sense of national interests that we may hope to see emerge in more settled times—to take too negative and constricted a view of future U.S. attitudes toward national security. Specifically, it would probably be a mistake to assume that the United States will permanently isolate itself from the attempts of foreign countries to maintain their independence and freedom from the kind of domination imposed through outside intervention that we have witnessed in Angola.

Security Policies—Defense, Deterrence, and Détente. At the level of military and security policy, important shifts are occurring, the full reach of which cannot yet be discerned. By far the most important cause of these shifts, which have profoundly altered the form and substance of world strategic relationships, has been the development in large numbers of thermonuclear weapons that are accurate, reliable, survivable, and devastatingly destructive. This development has been reflected in a shift from the simpler concept of defense, the actual waging of war for the safeguarding of our security interests, toward policies first of deterrence, then of détente, and now toward a complex interlacing of defense, deterrence, and détente in highly sophisticated combination. No one or two of these alone will provide us adequate and economical means of attaining security. All three are necessary if our security posture is to be effective and sensible. The task for top-level civilian and military leadership, the secretary of defense and the Joint Chiefs of Staff in particular, is to define and develop the role of each correctly.

In the area of defense, the actual wartime conduct of military operations, attention centers above all on the countering of any actual Soviet nuclear attack. Regarding the validity of this objective there is a wide measure of agreement and common understanding. But the means and concepts for accomplishing it, whether through massive retaliatory attacks, or selective counterforce operations, are subject to continual evolution and receive the close, collaborative attention of planning staffs and decision makers, civil and military.

A second great responsibility in case of war would be the conduct of regional, theater-type defense operations. In the North

Atlantic area, both at sea and in Europe, and in the Pacific and the area of Japan and Korea, large-scale operations involving land, sea, and air forces, conventional and possibly nuclear as well, could be quickly initiated. The planning for the kinds of operations that would be conducted in each area is intricate and detailed, with necessity for political and military interaction at every stage, from the laying down of political objectives and policy guidelines (for the use of tactical nuclear weapons, for example) to the programming of stocks of ammunition and fuel, and the basing and deploying of U.S. and allied forces.

Planning for the possibility of smaller-scale operations elsewhere in the world—the protection of lines of communication and commerce on the seas, the provision of aid to threatened allies determined to preserve their freedom—is the third major category of possible defense tasking. Here the overriding requirement is for maximum flexibility, since no one can predict in specific detail just how such requirements might arise. The need for common understanding of military capabilities and of the range of political decisions that might commit military forces to action again draws military and civil leadership into close collaboration.

These are the broad patterns of defense preparation for countering actual attack, for waging war. Our military forces today have a high level of capability and are maintained at a high state of readiness to respond to a call for action. Yet the measure of protection they could give our people is, at best, decidedly limited and incomplete. Civil and military alike on both sides of the Iron Curtain cannot ignore the fact that in nuclear war hundreds of millions might die, while in theater-type war in Europe heavy devastation east and west of the Iron Curtain would be sustained and in other areas of the world heavy losses and severe setbacks to social and economic development would be likely to occur.

The strong, ready military forces and the skill and will to use them if necessary that provide us with the capability for actual warfighting are at the same time an indispensable underpinning for both the other major lines of security policy, deterrence and détente. Accordingly they must be carefully shaped by civil and military leadership to support these policies.

Deterrence, as it concerns civil and military leaders today, involves far more than the dissuasion of actual Soviet attack, whether in the form of nuclear attack, the classical all-out assault across Western Europe, the engulfment of West Berlin, or the execution of threats against critical third areas of the world. These and other actions against Western forces and territories have been and are being successfully deterred, but along with them any substantial or successful Soviet use of the threat of military force for purposes of intimidation or coercion is also being deterred. Essential to this deterrent effect are the military forces in being that are maintained by the West, particularly by the United States, and the resulting Soviet perception of the costs and risks that any aggression on their part would encounter.

The fundamentals of deterrence are, on our side, a defense capability and the will to use it if necessary, and on the Soviet side the belief that this capability and this will do in fact exist. To the extent that the Soviet leaders believe this, as they appear to believe it today in Europe, for example, they themselves make the decision not to attempt military action or even the threat of military action in order to obtain their international ends.

Détente, the third main line of security policy, is designed, in its military aspects, not so much to deter the threat as to reduce and even partially remove it—by reducing forces, by reducing the causes for conflict, by lessening the chances of uncontrolled and undesirable escalation or accidental provocations and miscalculations, and by building up a stake on both sides in the continuation of peace and of peaceful commerce between the Soviet Union and ourselves.

Détente, as the continuing arguments over its meaning tell us, is by no means a clear and self-explanatory concept, interpreted identically by the United States and the Soviet Union. The concept of détente needs to be considered by civil and military leaders in a more differentiated way than has sometimes been the case, under such headings as, first of all, the strategic nuclear force capabilities of the two sides, second, the security arrangements related to NATO and to Japan, third, security issues related to other areas of the world, and finally, the security benefit for the United States that can be expected to derive from Soviet interests in such measures as agreements on economic, technological, political, and cultural activities and exchanges.

The SALT negotiations have been the focus of détente in the matter of strategic nuclear forces and seem likely to remain so. Already, the resulting agreements are shaping and constraining the future nuclear capabilities of the United States and the U.S.S.R. Every type of strategic weapon is being examined for its implications with meticulous care, for these are forces that give to each country that possesses them the power to threaten the national survival of any other. While the main thrust of the negotiations has been quantitative—that is, the limitation of numbers of land-based, sea-based, and airborne missiles, aircraft and the like—qualitative improvements, such as multiple warheads, are also being deliberated. Likewise, provisions for U.S.-Soviet consultations aimed at heading off dangerous confrontations seem certain to continue to receive high priority in this field of détente.

Détente applies as well to regional defense arrangements, such as those in Europe. Here its influence, already significant, seems likely to increase through, above all, the Mutual and Balanced Force Reductions (MBFR) negotiations that have been under way in Vienna for the last two years. By such negotiations, the participants are testing whether the processes of mutual force limitations that have been demonstrated in SALT can also be applied to military forces below the strategic nuclear level, particularly ground forces. The Conference on Security and Cooperation in Europe, concluded in 1975, covered topics such as major military movements and large-scale training exercises.

The motivation of the Soviet Union and the Western countries to reach agreement in the MBFR negotiations is noticeably weaker than it has been in SALT. The interests involved in MBFR, though vital to both sides, are thought to be less dangerously poised in terms of their potential for suddenly triggering nuclear attacks, and the forces involved—ground forces, chiefly—are much more diverse and much harder to quantify in terms that are common to the two sides. Nevertheless, the issues are still of very great long-term importance; they affect, for example, the degree of the Soviet Union's military predominance over its allies in Eastern Europe. And they are unquestionably going to be dealt with cautiously and deliberately by our military and civilian authorities.

In third areas of the world, such as the Middle East, the interests of the two sides do not seem to clash directly enough to create quite the same motivation for seeking or establishing mutual agreements. There are issues of high interest to both the United States and the U.S.S.R. in these areas, but they do not touch directly on questions of short-term national survival. While the two superpowers seem likely to continue to try to work out understandings and accords and to avoid high-intensity confrontation, each will try, in addition, to advance its interests separately with the countries in question. In these third areas of the world, the Soviet leaders have made it very clear that to them détente does *not* imply ideological peaceful coexistence. In simple terms, they wish to retain their freedom to expand—to strengthen the Soviet presence and influence, to extend the Soviet system and the Brezhnev Doctrine in ways that will bring additional nations into what they call the Socialist camp. Threats to peace and order will continue to occur in these third areas of the world, along with occasional pulling and hauling by both the United States and the U.S.S.R., to which civil and military authorities must respond. Our military forces have to be designed, equipped, and trained accordingly.

The final area of détente having military implications is the security benefit that may accrue to us as a by-product of economic, technological, political, and cultural agreements, by which the U.S.S.R. sets great store, through their "linkage" effects. Thus far experience suggests that it will be wise to pursue a somewhat cautious approach in this domain. There is little to indicate that such benefits will be very strong or dependable, even though the Soviet leaders may want some of the economic and technological benefits that the United States could extend to them under the umbrella of détente. This will be a matter for continuing debate and reevaluation among our people, in our Congress, and within civilian and military circles in the executive branch.

Major Military Tasks. The military tasks that derive from the requirements of these three major lines of policy (defense, deterrence, and détente) may be considered in three main groups: strategic nuclear tasks, regional tasks, and tasks that are of a global nature or relate to critical areas where American interests are likely to be importantly engaged in the time ahead.

The strategic nuclear task requires the United States to design, deploy, and steadfastly modernize an adequate, ready, responsive, reliable, and survivable nuclear counterforce to the tremendously powerful nuclear force—ICBM, SLBM, and aircraft—that the Soviet Union arrays against us. It is the unending responsibility of our military establishment to build, train, control, and (should such ever be necessary) utilize this force in combat operations. The size and composition of these strategic nuclear forces, particularly in relation to the size and composition of the forces of the Soviet Union, is an enduring issue, on which the most skillful and sophisticated intellectual analysis, embracing the whole range of political and military aspects of the problem, must be brought to bear.

In the second category of military tasks—the regional tasks—the prime example, of course, is Europe. The basic aim here is simply to deny the territory of Western Europe to the Soviet Union in case of attack; the secondary aim, to do what can be done to limit the destructive effects such an attack would have on Western Europe. In every way possible, the Soviet Union must be brought to realize that an attack on one NATO nation would indeed be an attack on all. This consideration is the reason for being of [the] integrated military commands in Europe, to which national forces of nearly all of the NATO members are committed.

The need for a collective, multinational solution to the regional security task poses requirements of great complexity in working out the specific defense arrangements for the area. International agreement must be achieved, both in principle and in practice, on all essential aspects of such arrangements. The NATO strategy, for example, involves forward defense, flexibility of response, collectivity of response, and undetermined duration of conflict—each one a subject filled with the potential for disagreement or for uncoordinated unilateral action on the part of participating nations. One needs only to mention the whole knotty subject of arms standardization, with its complex military and commercial implications, to demonstrate that the intellectual demands on senior responsible officials are indeed substantial.

Extending beyond NATO are such further military tasks as helping to safeguard the security of Japan; preventing foreign military intervention and the introduction of hostile or foreign military forces into Latin America; providing support and reassurance to other areas of the world, such as Australia and New Zealand, key areas of the Middle East, Indonesia, and the Philippines; maintaining freedom of the seas; giving support, when so directed, to the independence and sovereignty of free nations of the world threatened from outside; and maintaining the capability of intervention in areas of the world that our highest political authority may deem sufficiently critical to the security interests of the United States to justify such intervention in time of crisis. This is a full and demanding agenda for our security authorities and for their supporting staffs. A single issue, the current negotiations on revisions to the law of the sea, shows how important and difficult their work can be.

Three broad observations can be made at this point regarding these military tasks and requirements:

(1) The need will continue for strong forces in being, maintained in a high state of readiness and supported by programs of modernization and reequipment that will keep them qualitatively on a par with, or preferably ahead of, those of any competitor, specifically, the Soviet Union.

(2) There are critical linkages and interfaces that must be effectively managed by the high leadership of our defense establishment. To correlate high-level policy with military strategy and military posture will require effective and mutually supportive relations between civilians and top military authority, as well as good functional arrangements between our services—army, navy, air force, marines—in their capacity as the providers of the military forces and resources needed for security, and the joint and unified command structures that guide their employment and their readiness.

(3) Given the complexity and vital importance of these tasks, there is exceptional need for high quality, personal integrity, and dedication in the people who man, lead, and manage these military forces and the defense establishment. It is ultimately upon their dedication, their personal qualities, their skill, and their informed understanding of the issues involved that the successful accomplishment of these tasks must depend.

Force Development. The task of building and rebuilding the forces and shaping and reshaping the whole military establishment needed to fulfill the requirements that flow from these far-flung and important tasks is one of the foremost responsibilities of military officers and men and their civilian superiors. To meet these needs, units are formed, their higher direction is organized, support facilities and functions are provided, and training systems are established and operated. While continuity and stability are sought, constant change —contraction, expansion, revision, redirection—is necessarily characteristic of every aspect of the work of the military, from recruitment of personnel to procurement of equipment.

By presidential and congressional decision, obviously reflecting our leaders' interpretations of public preferences, ours are now voluntary forces. Our experience with voluntary recruitment is still limited: we have not yet completed a full cycle of prosperity-recession-prosperity since the system was adopted. Some of the problems that the future will bring are probably still masked by the pressures of civilian unemployment, pressures that fall heavily on young people eligible for military service. Initially, when the voluntary system was instituted, intensive well-supported programs were begun to stimulate enlistment, and a great deal of command attention was brought to bear on the problem. Nevertheless, recruitment fell significantly short of the target levels and, despite earlier assurances by high officials to the contrary, quality standards were quickly reduced. As the recession bit deeper, enlistment rates and quality standards rose. At the same time, however, cutbacks were ordered in enlistment incentives and in recruiting services. What the result will be as employment possibilities improve is, of course, uncertain. If unemployment stays in the 7 to 8 percent range, with heavy impact still falling on young people seeking to establish themselves, the appeal of a military tour to learn a skill, gain organizational experience and broadened horizons, and build a financial base will undoubtedly remain strong.

The educational requirements implied by a volunteer force—understanding it, attracting it, and administering it—range from social sensitivity and managerial efficiency to the hard skills that most of the recruits will be seeking to obtain.

A powerful military establishment such as our own must provide its personnel with modern materiel, military equipment and supplies of all kinds. The life cycle of such materiel, from conception through research and development, adoption and procurement, introduction as an operational capability, maintenance and modification, to final retirement or replacement, now extends to twenty-five years or more. In Europe, the aircraft planned for replacement of the F-104 aircraft (itself introduced in the 1950s) is expected still to be in service in the year 2000. Yet the premium on rapid innovation in major new technologies—the laser, for example—can be extremely high. This factor is especially important to us, since the expansionist urge lies with the other side. Technological superiority is a decisive margin that can never be conceded to a potential aggressor.

At every stage of the equipment life cycle, the educational requirements, though differing in content, are alike in their importance. There is a crucial but difficult interaction between technician and operator by which each must comprehend enough of the other's expertise to arrive at joint determinations as to what technical innovations might be both beneficial and practicable. The decision to adopt a particular item of equipment and the schedule for its adoption likewise require dual judgments as to cost and effectiveness, in which the military men who will employ the system and the civilian authorities, executive and congressional, who will weigh the improvement in terms of policy and funding must be capable of interacting constructively with each other. Finally, the determination of obsolesence, the decision whether to rebuild or replace, requires informed managerial judgments and processes in which both civilian and military sectors must participate.

In each of these phases, the need for advanced educational activity extending from research to teaching is readily apparent. The sums of money involved are large. The problems parallel some of the most crucial for civilian enterprises. And the policy implications, both domestic and foreign, are of the first order. We need only reflect on the issues of the MIRV, the cruise missile, and the Backfire bomber to realize how important to peace and stability they can be. The careful preparation of responsible military and civilian officials is indispensable.

Modern military forces are highly dependent upon supporting facilities—air bases, naval bases, army casernes, logistic depots, protected command installations and communications, hundreds of costly installations of many kinds. Within our own country, the decisions concerning such facilities reflect everything from military need and operationally advantageous location to the availability of transportation and labor and seniority and the influence of key members of congressional committees. A constant give-and-take between opposing interests lies behind these decisions; service efforts to reduce or eliminate less productive facilities frequently clash with congressional opposition to cutbacks harmful to a particular congressman's district. The range of considerations is, to say the least, interdisciplinary, and the need for knowledgeable treatment of the issues, in a context of good will and understanding of the political process, without sacrifice of the dictates of economy and effectiveness, calls for education in complex forms of management analysis and decision making.

The functioning of the military establishment—men, materiel, and facilities, once mobilized and organized—is no less demanding. In recent years at the managerial level the techniques of planning, programming, and budgeting have received great emphasis. To these must be added consideration of policy, since it is policy that gives direction and purpose to the whole effort; without an adequate subservience to policy, the military enterprise tends to drift off toward ends of its own. The linkage of high-level policy with military plans and programs, which requires, ideally, greater clarity about policy than has often been evidenced in Washington in recent years, is in fact one of the weakest points in the provision of rational, responsive government in the field of military affairs. This requirement is dauntingly complex. The most advanced academic and intellectual insights are no more than a necessary starting point. The ability to base practical decisions on such insights, within a framework of tested and refined concepts, is indispensable to coherent policy. It is a task that requires a certain measure of intellectual humility, combined with resolute determination and readiness to make decisions when required, even when the available evidence is incomplete and unconfirmed. The scholar's careful respect for what we do not know can be of great value, as can the whole body of knowledge and experience that is known as military professionalism.

The effective command of complex military units and organizations remains as much an art as a science. Development of the capacity for exercising command effectively is advanced by studies ranging from history and the understanding of the human condition to ethics and the psychology of leadership, before the processes of decision, the capabilities of weapons, the elements of alliance relationships, the thought patterns, culture, and doctrine of possible opponents, and the whole gamut of professional military knowledge are even broached. Whether giving advice to higher authority, responding to the Congress, informing the public, working in harmony with the civilian institutions and sectors of our society, directing and managing subordinate units and echelons, or guiding and drawing maximum support from his own headquarters and staff, a modern senior commander has need of every aid that will broaden, deepen, and soundly ground his understanding of his responsibilities and the methods by which he can fulfill them. As he rises in rank and responsibility, the commander, like his principal staff members, concentrates on understanding his mission and the means appropriate to its fulfillment that combine effectiveness with economy and acceptability, that is, conformity to the values and tenets of our society.

Particularly in intelligence and operational planning activities, command staffs must rely upon essentially military education and experience. Yet even these activities touch importantly on civilian concerns. Intelligence requires, in addition to careful, sustained development of sources and methods, the building up and constant updating of a vast and varied body of knowledge regarding possible adversaries, particularly their military forces. It is an area especially vulnerable to spasmodic intervention by higher authority and to the compromise of sources and methods. The damaging exposures resulting from the recent investigations by the Congress into intelligence activities prove nothing so much as the need for the intelligence community to avoid, in the future, transgressions and excesses that might occasion another round of revelations of this kind.

In the case of operational planning, the need is not only, as suggested earlier, to align planning with higher policy, but also to find valid military solutions within the parameters set by such policies. Within alliances, the process is exceptionally complex, since even agreement upon a form of words—NATO's strategy of "flexible response," for example, or the doctrine concerning the use of tactical nuclear weapons—may mask differing interests and national positions that more detailed planning will bring to the fore. And in the third world the need to preserve a capacity for responding in ways that cannot be predicted in specific detail forces the military planner to study carefully, together with their underlying causes and constraints, a wide spectrum of arrangements for the organization and employment of forces.

Educational Patterns. The educational preparation to meet these needs necessarily falls into a wide range of categories. Institutional need or motivation for such education is only part of the story. A large measure of individual choice, interest, and motivation must also be allowed for if the aim is to be achieved, since ultimate success or failure in anything so personal as education depends heavily upon the attitude of the individual, especially at the more advanced levels. The aim of self-development is a strand that runs through the wide diversity of educational programs in which American servicemen and women are engaged. It combines in varying degrees with the more strictly institutional need in shaping the specific programs pursued by individuals. Nevertheless, it is possible to assess most of the effort as primarily institutionally motivated, with of course a large and essential component of individual motivation. A lesser, though still highly important, volume of primarily individually motivated education also takes place, from which the military establishment receives very substantial direct and indirect benefits.

For officers, the institutionally motivated education principally includes:

> (1) Officer acquisition education and training, including, in particular, ROTC participation, education at the service academies, and special programs such as that for medical doctors.
>
> (2) Progressive military education, extending from basic courses through more advanced command and staff courses to attendance for selected officers at the service war colleges.
>
> (3) Specialized and functional courses in such fields as technology, intelligence, languages, and management.
>
> (4) Advanced academic education, often culminating in the master's or doctor's degree, as preparation for serving in high-level staff or command positions or on the faculty of a military educational institution (such as the service academies).

For enlisted men and women, the corresponding education and training includes:

(1) Recruit training, the achievement of the abilities necessary for effective participation in a military unit.

(2) Skill training, the development of specialized capabilities in the vast number of occupational assignments that comprise the military establishment.

(3) More advanced leadership training for senior noncommissioned officers and others with managerial duties.

The educational programs that are primarily individually motivated fall principally, for officers and enlisted personnel alike, in the area of degree-completion programs, buttressed by general educational development programs and other arrangements for individual activity.

Major Educational Programs

A brief review of the major programs now under way will give an indication of the scope and nature of the educational activities of the military forces.

In fiscal year 1976, the total "training load" in the active military forces—for individual training and education of military personnel, officer and enlisted, related both to accession or entry into military service and to later, more advanced instruction—amounted to approximately 230,000 individuals.[1] Some 75 percent of these—roughly 175,000—were engaged in the "accession-related" phase, covering recruit training, initial skill training, undergraduate flight training or familiarization, and officer acquisition training. The remainder—over 55,000—were engaged in development of other skills and in other flight training as well as in the process of professional development, which continues throughout a military career.

It is of interest that nearly 25,000 personnel received comparable training for the reserve forces the same year, nearly 10,000 of them engaged in recruit training, and some 14,000 in training in specialized skills.

Officer acquisition training, a function that is crucially important to the future health and effectiveness of the forces, was being given to some 18,000 individuals of the active and reserve forces in FY 1976, not including ROTC training (in which average enrollment in FY 1976 amounted to 67,350). The service academies, meanwhile, were

---

[1] Department of Defense, *Military Manpower Training Report for FY 1976*, March 1975, p. v.

Table 3-1

EDUCATION AND TRAINING, ACTIVE FORCES, FISCAL YEAR 1976

(in thousands of man-years)

Accession-related education and training	
Recruit training	66.1
Officer acquisition[a]	17.5
Initial skill (enlisted and officer)	85.9
Undergraduate flight training	4.8
Subtotal	174.3
Subsequent education and training	
Specialized skill	41.0
Other flight training	0.8
Professional development	14.2
Subtotal	56.0
Total, active forces	230.3

[a] Does not include ROTC.
Source: Department of Defense, *Military Manpower Training Report for FY 1976*, March 1975, p. v.

educating a total of somewhat over 12,000 students. Officer candidate schools (approximately 1,200 average load) and other enlisted commissioning programs, many of them in engineering and management, with an average enrollment of some 1,900, accounted for the bulk of the remainder. There were also "health professionals acquisition programs," with an annual average training load of 1,500 individuals.[2]

The variety of programs by which college men and women can gain entry into military service is well described in the publication, "Pathways in Military Service for College Men and Women," issued by the Department of Defense.[3] It lists a hundred different programs in current use, the greatest diversity being in the medical and related fields but numerous others being in chaplaincy and in legal and other professional fields, as well as the ROTC and service academy programs previously mentioned.

[2] Ibid., pp. IV-2–IV-12.
[3] Office of the Assistant Secretary of Defense (Manpower and Reserve Affairs), April 1974.

Table 3-2
PROFESSIONAL DEVELOPMENT EDUCATION, ACTIVE FORCES, FISCAL YEAR 1976
(in thousands of man-years)

Basic officers' professional schools[a]	0.8
Intermediate service schools	1.8
Senior service colleges	0.8
Enlisted leadership training	0.5
Graduate education[b]	3.3
At service institutions[c]	(1.4)
Other degree-completion programs	3.5
Other full-time education (nondegree programs)	1.1
Health professionals	2.5
	14.3

[a] Servicewide courses; more specific courses are included under specialized skill training.
[b] For validated billets (that is, positions designated by the Department of Defense as warranting an incumbent with graduate-level education).
[c] Naval Postgraduate School and Air Force Institute of Technology.
Source: Department of Defense, *Military Manpower Training Report*, pp. VII-2–VII-16.

More immediately related to the broad range of military tasks that involve close civil-military relations and collaboration are the programs for continuing and progressive professional development of our military personnel. The skill-progression training of enlisted personnel includes more than 3,000 different courses of widely varying duration and content, with a total average annual training load of 24,000 individuals. For officers, the courses number more than 2,500, and the annual training load comes to more than 20,000.[4] By any standard, these are substantial developmental undertakings, essential to the attainment of the level and diversity of technical and professional skills upon which our services depend.

The programs included under "Professional Development Education" are by far the most directly significant for the kinds of staff and command responsibilities examined earlier.

Within this overall effort, officer professional development courses at three levels—basic, intermediate, and senior—compose a first set of

---
[4] Department of Defense, *Military Manpower Training Report*, pp. V-2–V-15.

subcategories. At the basic level, professional development courses not already cited under specialized skills involve a training load of some 800 officers at certain Marine Corps and air force schools. For the intermediate courses at the staff and command schools the load amounts to just under 2,000 officers, and at the senior service colleges the load comes to just over 800. There are, in addition, enlisted leadership schools for senior noncommissioned officers that have an average annual load of between 400 and 500.

In addition to these courses of study, the numerous programs in civilian institutions and at the graduate level at the Naval Postgraduate School and the Air Force Institute of Technology provide high-quality education in many fields. The annual average for validated billets (that is, positions designated by the Department of Defense as warranting an incumbent with graduate education) at graduate institutions now runs at some 3,300, including nearly 1,900 at civilian institutions, almost 1,000 at the Naval Postgraduate School, and nearly 500 at the Air Force Institute of Technology. More than 21,000 billets in all in the Department of Defense have been identified as requiring education at the graduate level.

The services support other degree completion programs as well, in which in FY 1976 an average of 850 individuals are seeking graduate degrees and some 1,600 are working for other degrees. Other full-time education in a wide variety of scientific, administrative, and other fields is conducted both in civilian institutions and in Department of Defense schools, often in courses of short duration. With an average of just over 1,000 attending at any one time, the total "output" now runs to more than 11,000 each year. Finally, education for health professionals adds a further 2,500 annual average to the total, giving an aggregate of approximately 14,000 in this crucially important effort.[5]

The result of all this, as pointed out in a recent study by a panel of the National Academy of Public Administration,[6] is an officer corps in the military services reflecting "the broad national trends toward increased levels of education in the general population and in other executive groups." The report goes on to say,

> The proportion of officers who are college graduates rose from 47 percent in 1952 to 76 percent in 1971. A college degree is now accepted as the minimal basic educational

---
[5] Department of Defense, *Military Manpower Training Report*, pp. VII-2–VII-16.
[6] "Military Officer Graduate Education—Achieving Excellence with Economy," A Report of a Panel of the National Academy of Public Administration, May 23, 1975, Washington, D.C.

qualification for entering officers. Many also hold graduate or professional degrees acquired before or after entering the services. In 1973, an estimated 45,000 or 15 percent had one or more graduate degrees: 41,600, a master's, and 3,800, a doctorate. In addition about 28,000 held postbaccalaureate professional degrees in medicine, dentistry, nursing, other health fields, law, and the ministry. As the armed services are a relatively self-contained institution with distinctive functions, they cannot be compared precisely to other American institutions. However, the incidence of graduate education in the officer corps, and its distribution, rising with rank, appears to be roughly comparable to that of the executive force in industry and government. In the panel's opinion, this is as it should be.[7]

In 1973, preentry education accounted for 17 percent of the estimated 45,000 graduate degrees, or just over 7,500; in-service education for the remainder, with some 25,000 of the total resulting from fully funded (that is, government-financed) programs. Off-duty courses, cooperative arrangements between service schools and private institutions, degree-completion programs, and other methods such as Rhodes scholarships and National Science Foundation fellowships produced an estimated 12,500 graduate degrees in 1973.[8]

Many of these degrees are the result of just a small part—though a most important one—of the massive voluntary education program of the armed forces. This is a set of many subprograms in which about 575,000 part-time students were engaged in 1974, supported by Department of Defense operating costs in excess of $50 million. In 1973, some 78,000 military personnel were engaged in high school completion, 6,000 in two-year college completion, 2,000 working for a baccalaureate, another 2,000 for a master's degree, and 20 for a doctorate. This is a dynamic area, in which recent developments in the form of cooperative arrangements with civilian institutions are proving of major benefit to educational and career opportunities for men and women in uniform.[9] Total funding for military education programs for FY 1976—including officer acquisition, professional development and support of voluntary education—has reached a total in the range of $1 billion per year.[10] This educational endeavor will remain vast, diversified, and crucially important in the time ahead,

---

[7] Ibid., pp. II-1 and II-2.

[8] Ibid., pp. IV-2 and IV-3.

[9] Department of Defense, *A Summary of Voluntary Education in the Armed Forces*, May 3, 1974.

[10] DOD, *Military Manpower Training Report for FY 1976*, pp. X-2 and X-3.

but its very size, complexity, dynamism, and importance make clear that it will require close attention and wise guidance.[11]

Broad Issues Ahead

First among the issues meriting our continuing close concern as we look to the future are the linkages between the military establishment, the higher echelons of government, and the society at large. In a time of rapid change, the process of educating succeeding generations of officers in the nature and substance of civil-military relations will be unrelenting in its demands. Its aim must be a shared, informed understanding on both sides, military and civilian alike, that links professional military skill with the values, political priorities, and decisions of civil authority and the people at large. The challenges to military leadership will inevitably be severe. High-quality, broadly based education will be essential to dealing with them in a way that meets security needs, while at the same time measuring up to other civilian policies, goals, and constraints.

The quest for excellence, which has been the task of the Department of Defense Committee on Excellence in Education, headed by the deputy secretary of defense, must go on without interruption. It is a useful emphasis and a useful reminder that counterpressure must constantly be exerted to see that shorter-term constraints do not drain the military education process of its vitality and scope. The military services, and particularly their top career leadership, hold special responsibilities in this regard. They must deal with the problem on a long-term, broad-gauged basis extending well beyond the inevitably shorter focus of the ever-changing civilian leadership within the executive branch. The continuity of congressional committees helps to offset tendencies within the executive branch and Congress that, all too naturally, emphasize short-term payoffs in weighing educational benefits against their financial costs. Wisdom demands a tolerance for broader studies within the framework of the basic requirements of civil-military relationships. It is precisely such studies that equip future leaders to surmount the tendencies toward bureaucratization and mediocritization that are ever-present in a big institution of

---

[11] A number of groups have been giving the program their close scrutiny in the recent past: the NAPA panel, already mentioned; the General Accounting Office (Comptroller General of the United States, *Report to the Congress: Improvements Needed in Determining Graduate Education Requirements for Military Officers Positions*, August 28, 1970); and the DOD Committee on Excellence in Education, chaired by Deputy Secretary of Defense Clements.

this kind and to provide fresh approaches to emerging changes and new problems.

Education of the highest order will be needed to grapple with unsolved problems of American security—those now unsolved, such as an adequate yet supportable security policy toward the Third World, and those that will arise as stable relationships now existing are eroded or altered by new technological discoveries and applications or by shifts in the strength or alignment of nations. The vast and complex challenges that will surely confront us will demand a high ethic of dedication to our national ideals and goals, of self-development toward maximum individual contribution, and of selfless service in support of the attainment of our security objectives and interests. In its very process as well as in its results—the search for truth that characterizes the world of learning and the deeper understanding of the tenets of free societies that it affords—education can help us meet these needs.

Finally, education itself can help restore mutual respect and understanding between the world of education and the world of military strength and vigilance. The deterioration in the relations between the two that has been suffered in recent years is incompatible with the needs of a healthy democratic society—a society in which both are indispensable, both should be indissolubly identified with the parent society, and both must work in harmony.

The educational processes that contribute so much to the effective and successful working out of our civil-military relations form a carefully designed, highly refined, intricately coordinated structure of competence and responsiveness. It is well managed and closely supervised. It needs steadfast support, continuing innovation and vitalization, and wise, broad-visioned leadership in order to continue to make its vital contribution to national security and well-being.

3
A CASE STUDY OF CIVIL-MILITARY RELATIONS: ETHIOPIA

Gene A. Sherrill

Morris Janowitz stated in 1964 that "the authoritarian-personal type of control, as in the case of Ethiopia, is a format which cannot produce the conditions for modernization and which seems certain to be swept aside by some form of collective leadership—civilian or, more likely, military."[1] Janowitz's assessment proved accurate. On September 12, 1974, over 2,000 years of imperial rule in Ethiopia ended with the deposition of Emperor Haile Selassie I and the establishment of a provisional military government.

How and why did the military intervene? In order to answer this question we must study first the complex and gradual development of the relationship between civilian authority and the armed forces in Ethiopia.

Historical View

The Traditional Past. The long history of Ethiopia prior to 1855, when the modern monarchy began, was characterized by tribal integration, the establishment of the Solomonic Dynasty, the development of Christianity, the evolution of a feudal nobility, and the growth of a military culture—all of which influenced the political, economic, social, and cultural conditions that would emerge in the twentieth century and lead to intervention by the military.

Ethiopia had its beginnings in the migration of Semitic tribes from Arabia to the highlands of the African horn during the first

---

[1] Morris Janowitz, *The Military in the Political Development of New Nations: An Essay in Comparative Analysis* (Chicago: University of Chicago Press, 1964), p. 103.

millenium before Christ.[2] These tribes merged with the local Cushitic tribes to found the Kingdom of Aksum, a city-state contemporaneous with Imperial Rome. From this union evolved two of the three ethnic groups dominant in Ethiopia today—the Amhara and the Tigre. Internal conflict and religious wars weakened the position of the various emperors during the sixteenth century and precipitated the replacement of imperial power with feudal political arrangements. From the south, meanwhile, Ethiopia was invaded by a third major ethnic group, the Galla. Had the Galla not been so divided among themselves, they might well have become the politically dominant ethnic group.[3] Instead, however, they settled in the southern regions of the empire and began a slow process of assimilation that is still going on. Today the Galla comprise about 40 percent of the population and are the largest ethnic group; the Amhara and Tigre form the elite minority with a little more than 30 percent of the population; and the remainder of the population consists of some forty other tribes and peoples.[4]

According to Robert L. Hess, the Solomonic Dynasty "has been the single most important factor in the emergence of Ethiopia as a modern state in the past century."[5] Legend has it that the dynasty of Ethiopian kings can be traced back to a union between King Solomon and Makeda, the queen of Sheba, which produced a son. This son, Menelik I, later became king of Aksum. Subsequent rulers including Haile Selassie claimed descent from Menelik to help legitimize their positions as emperors, and Article 2 of Ethiopia's Revised Constitution of 1955 institutionalized this tradition.[6]

An important factor in the development of Ethiopian culture and political environment was the conversion to Christianity, which probably occurred during the fourth century A.D.[7] The Ethiopian Orthodox Church, although threatened by the spread of Islam, internal strife, and religious wars, survived and emerged by the fourteenth century as the strongest integrating force in Ethiopian society and the

---

[2] Margery Perham, *The Government of Ethiopia*, 2nd ed. (Evanston: Northwestern University Press, 1969), p. 10.

[3] Robert L. Hess, *Ethiopia: The Modernization of Autocracy* (Ithaca, N.Y.: Cornell University Press, 1970), p. 48.

[4] Peter Schwab, ed., *Ethiopia and Haile-Selassie* (New York: Facts on File, 1972), pp. 5-6.

[5] Hess, *Ethiopia*, p. xix.

[6] The text of the Revised Constitution of 1955 can be found in Perham, *Government of Ethiopia*, pp. 433-62.

[7] Richard Greenfield, *Ethiopia: A New Political History* (New York: Frederick A. Praeger, 1965), p. 24.

dominant element of an incipient national ideology.[8] By the middle of the twentieth century the church had become a major political force in Ethiopia: some 40 percent of the population were Christian and the church owned, tax-free, somewhere between 18 percent and 30 percent of the land.[9]

It was inevitable, considering the historical evolution of feudalism in Ethiopia, the nobility would emerge as another strong political influence. Tribal and ethnic fragmentation stratified society; this was a system "founded on authority, in which vertical lines of communication largely replace horizontal ones."[10] The prevailing modes of land tenure and landlord-tenant relations produced an agricultural society in which about 90 percent of the population still earn a living from farming or livestock.[11]

Ethiopian history is laden with records of military campaigns and chronic internecine warfare. Before the existence of a strong central government, members of the local nobility maintained their positions of authority by establishing their own loyal armies. A relationship similar to that between tenant and landlord evolved, since "all able-bodied adult males who were not members of the religious orders were expected to be soldiers if called to the service of their local lord."[12] Honors, favors, and political appointments were handed out as rewards for success in battle. Outstanding military achievement became a key to social mobility. Military culture occupied a prominent place in the overall pattern of Amhara-Tigre culture, so much so, in fact, that "the political involvement of the military is not a phenomenon that needs to be explained; on the contrary, any distinction between the two realms is difficult to make."[13] Thus, the military joined the monarchy, the church, and the nobility as one of the major forces in Ethiopia's drive toward modernization.

The Seeds of Modernization (1855–1930). Centralized power almost completely disappeared in Ethiopia during the hundred years before

---

[8] John Markakis, *Ethiopia: Anatomy of a Traditional Polity* (Oxford, England: Clarendon Press, 1974), p. 28.

[9] Schwab, *Ethiopia and Haile-Selassie*, p. 5.

[10] Christopher S. Clapham, *Haile-Selassie's Government* (New York: Frederick A. Praeger, 1969), p. 5.

[11] Schwab, *Ethiopia and Haile-Selassie*, p. 5.

[12] Irving Kaplan et al., *Area Handbook for Ethiopia* (Washington: U.S. Government Printing Office, 1971), p. 479.

[13] Donald N. Levine, "The Military in Ethiopian Politics: Capabilities and Constraints," in *The Military Intervenes: Case Studies in Political Development*, ed. Henry Bienen (New York: Russell Sage Foundation, 1968), p. 6.

1855. Nobles and regional rulers dominated a number of small kingdoms, and Ethiopia became a mere geographical expression. Four strong, innovative emperors, however—Theodore II, Yohannes IV, Menelik II, and Haile Selassie I—emerged to sow the seeds of modernization. Each in his own way attempted to create a national unity that would override earlier religious, ethnic, and regional differences. Notably, too, each claimed Solomonic descent to help legitimize his rule.[14]

Theodore II (1855–1868) made the first attempt to establish permanent administrative institutions within the empire. However, he was thwarted by a deeply entrenched Amhara and Tigrean aristocracy and was forced to rely on military strength to maintain control. He then attempted to import technological skills and weapons by proposing a treaty of commerce and friendship with Great Britain. The failure of this endeavor resulted in a British punitive expedition, which served as a catalyst for Theodore's deposition by the church, the Tigrean lords, and the lesser nobility.

After four years of civil war, Emperor Yohannes IV (1872–1889) emerged to continue Theodore's policies of restricting the power of the nobility. "Yohannes wanted to control the nobility and lay the basis for a state that could be called modern, but struggles with regional lords, Europeans, and Sudanese Muslims prevented him from achieving his goals." [15]

Menelik II (1889–1913) took the first successful steps toward modernization in Ethiopia. With a modernized army he curbed rival Italian expansionism, defeating the Italian army at Andowa in 1896. He also launched a campaign of territorial expansion, and by 1900 Ethiopia, with the exception of Italian Eritrea, had reached its present borders. Through skillful use of European advisers, Menelik further modernized Ethiopia's army, communications and transportation systems, and bureaucratic institutions. He maintained control by manipulating the nobility and encouraging traditional marriage connections within the Ethiopian aristocracy. His attempt to create the beginnings of a centralized ministerial government staffed by the forerunners of a modern elite had largely succeeded by 1906. However, failing health forced Menelik to name his grandson, Lij Iasu, as his successor in 1908 and instability reappeared.[16] Lij Iasu became emperor upon Menelik's death in 1913.

---

[14] Hess, *Ethiopia*, pp. 50-51.
[15] Ibid., p. 53.
[16] Lij, literally "child" or "boy," is an honorific title used for the sons of noble houses.

Lij Iasu proved to be a failure; when he publicly announced his conversion to Islam, the nobility, the church, and the army joined to overthrow him. After the successful coup, the various factions agreed that Ethiopia would be ruled by a triumvirate: Zawditu, Menelik's daughter, would reign as empress; Ras Tafari Makonnen of Harrar, a distant cousin of Menelik, would act as regent; and Habte Giorgis, a popular general, would remain as war minister, since he could control the army in the interests of the nobility.[17]

Between 1916 and 1930 Ras Tafari gradually extended his power by suppressing several rebellions while building his own small military force. The death of Habte Giorgis in 1926 and the suppression of an attempted coup in 1928 allowed him to exert greater influence on Zawditu and cleared the way for his accession to the throne when Zawditu died in 1930. He chose the throne name of Haile Selassie I. Haile Selassie had taken the first significant steps toward modernization before his succession, and he was now ready to build on those beginnings. In later years, however, he would find that the rate of modernization he supported was too slow for a developing political consciousness to tolerate.

Ethiopia under Haile Selassie (1930–1974). During the fourteen years preceding his coronation, Haile Selassie, in addition to consolidating his control, laid the foundations for modernizing Ethiopia. He strongly believed that education was the key to modernization; and, in addition to establishing schools around the country, he began sending young Ethiopians abroad to study, including some to the French military academy at Saint Cyr.[18] To establish a favorable position in the international arena, he won Ethiopia's admission to the League of Nations in 1923, emancipated Ethiopia's slaves in 1924, and made several trips abroad. These visits to the more advanced countries of the world strengthened Haile Selassie's belief that Ethiopia should modernize and prompted him to import foreign economic and technical advisers.[19]

In the five years before the Italian invasion in 1935, the emperor's principal contribution to modernization, as well as his most significant action to consolidate control, was the granting of the first Ethiopian

---

[17] Ras, literally "head," is a traditional military title often conferred upon the heads of important houses, provincial governors, ministers, and high officials. The military connotation is indicative of the military culture that developed over the long period of Ethiopia's history.
[18] Hess, *Ethiopia*, p. 65.
[19] Schwab, *Ethiopia and Haile-Selassie*, p. 3.

Constitution in 1931. Two deliberative bodies, a Senate and a Chamber of Deputies, were established. The Constitution also provided for a system of cabinet ministers that would form the basis for a modern bureaucratic administration. However, ultimate power remained, as it traditionally had, in the hands of the emperor. The Constitution was a feeble first step toward establishing political institutions, creating, in theory though not in practice, a separation of powers.[20] Haile Selassie continued to emphasize education by opening new elementary schools, sending students abroad to study, and establishing a military academy at Holeta near Addis Ababa in 1934.

Between 1935 and 1941 Ethiopia had its only experience with any form of colonialism. Using a relatively unimportant Ethiopian-Italian clash over a water hole as a pretext, Italy invaded and defeated Ethiopia, occupying the country for five years. The occupation proved costly for both Italy and Ethiopia. Resistance movements cost the Ethiopians several hundred members of their educated elite and hundreds of monks at the monastery of Debra Libanos, and many churches were burned. Italy, meanwhile, spent a fortune on roads, buildings, rail lines, and communication facilities during the occupation.[21]

Haile Selassie gained world prominence on June 30, 1936, when he presented an impassioned plea for the liberation of his country before the Assembly of the League of Nations in Geneva.[22] His plea fell on deaf ears and he went into exile, first in England until 1940 and then in Khartoum, Sudan. A joint force of British, Sudanese, and Ethiopians launched an attack in early 1941 and quickly routed the Italians. Haile Selassie returned to Addis Ababa on May 5, 1941.

Although the British demanded some concessions in repayment for their efforts, these were minimal; and full sovereignty was restored to Ethiopia in 1945. Haile Selassie lost no time in reestablishing his policy of political and administrative centralization and modernization. Between 1941 and 1944 he recalled the Parliament, set up a Council of Ministers (cabinet) as an advisory body to the emperor, established the office of prime minister, institutionalized levels of regional and local government under the authority of the central government, formed a police force and systemized judicial system, built up the army, initiated a system of land and income taxes, and

---

[20] The complete text of Emperor Haile Selassie's promulgation of the Constitution on July 16, 1931, and of the Constitution itself can be found in Perham, *Government of Ethiopia*, pp. 423-32.
[21] Schwab, *Ethiopia and Haile-Selassie*, p. 33.
[22] The text of Haile Selassie's address is printed in ibid., pp. 26-32.

stressed economic improvement. All of these actions were designed to consolidate his own centralized authority while reducing the power of the traditional elites, the church and the nobility.

The seven years or so after 1944 were fairly uneventful. Haile Selassie slowed his attempts at modernization to placate the conservative elements and to cement his position. A few minor provincial uprisings were crushed and several palace plots uncovered, the most serious being a planned coup to depose the emperor in 1947 and a plan to assassinate him in 1951.

Political conditions changed in the early 1950s. Domestic economic and educational programs were greatly expanded, and greater attention was given by Haile Selassie's government to national affairs. A new modernizing force began to emerge as the first postwar generation of Ethiopian students returned from schools abroad to take up positions in the government. In 1951 the University College of Addis Ababa was founded, and Ethiopian troops were dispatched to fight with United Nations forces in Korea. A year later the province of Eritrea was federated with Ethiopia by United Nations mandate. State visits to Europe and the United States in 1954 increased Ethiopia's contacts abroad. It was now time for a revision of the Constitution of 1931.

On the twenty-fifth anniversary of his accession to the throne, November 4, 1955, Haile Selassie promulgated the Revised Constitution of 1955. This was considerably longer than the earlier Constitution and "extended the roles of various political institutions, created new ones and carried further the effort to decentralize the central government." [23] Although the new Constitution seemed to increase the strength of modernizing elements, the authority of the emperor remained supreme. Significantly, the revisions recognized the legitimacy of the Solomonic Dynasty, provided for lineal succession, legitimized the Council of Ministers and the legislative bodies (Senate and Chamber of Deputies), expanded the powers of Parliament, and provided for popular election by electoral district of the members of the Chamber of Deputies. The role of the clergy was subordinated to the power of the emperor, though the archbishop of the Ethiopian Orthodox Church was made a member of the Crown Council, an advisory body to the emperor. The Constitution also gave Ethiopian workers the right to form or join associations, thus paving the way for the formation of labor unions in 1962. No provision was made for the evolution of political parties, but they were not specifically

---

[23] Ibid., p. 59.

banned. As it had after the promulgation of the first Constitution in 1931, paternal autocratic rule remained the keystone of government.[24]

In the next five years (1956–1960), Ethiopia elected a new Parliament, continued its tax reform efforts, and strengthened its relations with friendly nations. Haile Selassie made numerous trips abroad and entertained several heads of state. The United Nations Economic Commission for Africa was created in 1958 and established its headquarters in Addis Ababa, making that city an international center.

Nevertheless, a growing dissatisfaction with the rate of modernization and the beginning of a new political awareness were evident by 1960. University students, young civil servants, and recent graduates formed a small intellectual class that included labor leaders and members of the military. These young men favored more rapid modernization and talked of playing a greater role in national policy formulation.

On December 13, 1960, the frustrations growing within this small civilian and military elite were revealed in an attempted coup d'état. The coup was led by General Mangestu Neway, the commander of the Imperial Bodyguard (an elite force separate from the traditional Ethiopian military), and his radical brother, Germane, who had masterminded the plot. They were joined by the chiefs of police and security and a small segment of the political elite.[25]

The coup, staged while the emperor was on a state visit to Brazil, was initially successful in the capital. The rebels were able to capture the crown prince, Asfa Wossen, and more than twenty cabinet ministers and other important government leaders. But the coup lacked a solid base of support. Although the Imperial Bodyguard played a key role, its men and even the majority of its officers had not been informed of the purpose of the coup, and many of them actually thought they were fighting *for* the emperor. The rebels also failed to gain the support they had anticipated from the military as a whole, the students, and the Ethiopian Orthodox Church. The regular army, led by its commanders, remained loyal to the emperor, and in a few short days crushed the rebels as Haile Selassie returned to Addis Ababa. Before their defeat, however, the rebel leaders assassinated all but six of their captives and coerced the crown prince into publicly supporting their cause.

---

[24] "Ethiopia," *Foreign Affairs Review* (New Zealand), vol. 20 (March 1970), p. 8.
[25] Greenfield provides an exhaustive account of the coup d'état along with detailed biographical data on Mangestu and Germane Neway in *Ethiopia: New Political History*, pp. 337-452.

The exact aims of the rebels are difficult to identify. According to one source, their stated intent was the establishment of a government that would improve the economic, social, and political position of the masses by ending the rule of the aristocracy and instituting land reform.[26] These were not, per se, radical objectives. The rebels' aims showed a mixture of traditional and modernizing elements. There was no talk of constitutional reform, corruption, human rights, or elections since these themes would have instantly alienated the traditional elements in Ethiopian society.[27] Rather, the keynote of the charges against the imperial government was the relatively slow rate of progress in economic development, education, and living conditions.

Whatever its specific aims, the unsuccessful coup of 1960 had significant implications for Ethiopia's future. It gave a short but violent jolt to the modernizing process, illuminated the existing power bases of nobility, church, and armed forces within the imperial regime, provided the impetus for the growth of a political consciousness, and marked the beginning of the decline of the political strength of Haile Selassie. In 1961 and again in 1964 the military showed their increased political strength by enforcing demands for higher pay on a reluctant emperor. By 1968 university graduates had begun to occupy major government offices and were reaching higher ranks within the military. Slowly, the emperor began withdrawing from internal issues and turned instead to what seemed to him to be more pressing international problems. He still held his traditional power over the central government, but that power was beginning to weaken with time.

Eritrea, which had been federated with Ethiopia in 1952, became a province on November 14, 1962, by unanimous vote of the Ethiopian Parliament and the Eritrean Assembly.[28] Eritrean opponents of the decision rebelled and started a guerrilla movement, the Eritrean Liberation Front, to fight for Eritrean independence. This movement proved to be a source of internal unrest and division within Ethiopia and contributed to the eventual downfall of Haile Selassie.

Another vexing problem for the emperor during the 1960s was a border dispute with Somalia. The dispute centered on the unification with Somalia of migrant Somali tribes in southern Ethiopia. It was feared by the Ethiopian government that such unification, as

---

[26] Kaplan, *Area Handbook*, p. 68.
[27] Christopher S. Clapham, "The Ethiopian Coup d'Etat of December 1960," *Journal of Modern African Studies*, vol. 6 (1968), pp. 501-504.
[28] Schwab, *Ethiopia and Haile-Selassie*, p. 93.

well as an independent Eritrea, would produce secessionist tendencies in other provinces. Through extensive use of the military and political maneuvering in the Organization of African Unity, Haile Selassie succeeded in preventing unification.

The emperor intended to use the many young university graduates who had taken positions in government in the late 1960s as a force for modernization. However, these young bureaucrats had a different view of modernization from the emperor's. They were unhappy with the slow rate of progress and the general ineffectiveness of government. A product of Haile Selassie's emphasis on education, the students became a powerful political voice and aided in the decline of the emperor's power. Until 1960 the students appeared more loyal to the emperor than did the nobility, but by the time Haile Selassie had stripped most of the power from the land-holding aristocracy, the rising class of young educated people was becoming more and more dissatisfied with the traditional form of autocratic government. Their demands took shape gradually, centering on the contradictions between the rights granted by the Revised Constitution of 1955 and the limitations placed on those rights by the central government.[29] The students, both at home and abroad, began challenging government policies in the late 1960s. Student unrest finally came to a head in December 1969 when the president of the University Students' Union at the University of Haile Selassie was found shot to death.[30] This incident aroused the social and political conscience of the people of Ethiopia, particularly those in the urban centers.[31]

Several events and conditions developed during the early 1970s that were to bring about a major crisis in early 1974. Student agitation continued. Inflation had become a major problem, and rising prices led to discontent, strikes, and demonstrations. Even the army demonstrated for higher wages as a hedge against inflation. The emperor responded with a modest pay increase, but the military held out for more, a gesture of defiance that would have been unheard of only a few years earlier. Moral and financial corruption, widespread throughout the government, extended to local administrators who suppressed information revealing the seriousness of the drought and famine in Wollo and Tigre provinces in 1973. That tragedy drew the world's attention and within Ethiopia proved to be a crucial

---

[29] Hess, *Ethiopia*, pp. 166-67.
[30] Ibid., p. 172.
[31] Joseph S. Murphy and Tadesse Araya, "Innocent Emperor: Ethiopia Exploits Itself," *Nation*, vol. 219 (September 14, 1974), pp. 200-203.

emotional factor in the eventual overthrow of Haile Selassie. The entire political, social, and military environment was ripe for revolution.

The "Creeping Coup" (1974–1975).[32] The years of political, economic, social, and military instability, coupled with the gradual erosion of imperial power, came to a climax in February 1974, the month that marked the beginning of the deposition of Emperor Haile Selassie. The first stage of the coup started in mid-February and lasted until mid-April. It began with mutinies by junior officers and noncommissioned officers over their treatment by senior officers, employment conditions, pay, and the government's handling of drought relief in Wollo Province.[33] The climate of rebellion quickly spread to the civilian sector and resulted in student unrest, strikes, and protests by labor organizations over rising prices, corruption, and the drought and famine problems. The government failed to satisfy the various elements, and on February 28 the military forced the resignation of Prime Minister Akililu Habtewold and his cabinet. The emperor appointed a new government with Endalkachew Makonnen as prime minister.

From late February to mid-September "reformist elements within the ranks of the military moved to consolidate their power at the expense of the monarchy." [34] The military formed an internal political body of 120 members called the Armed Forces Committee, which later evolved into the Armed Forces Co-ordinating Committee, or *Dergue*. Finally, in September, the *Dergue* came to be known as the Provisional Military Administrative Council. These changes in name are indicative of the internal divisions and conflicts that existed within the military itself.

Whether by design or by compromise, the *Dergue* was successful in replacing the ruling monarchy with military rule without resorting to violence. They extracted concession after concession from Haile Selassie in the areas of constitutional reform, government appointments, and investigations of corruption and graft. Many of the most powerful figures in Ethiopia, including ministers, judges, government administrators, nobility, top military leaders, and the emperor's closest advisers, were arrested. Finally, the *Dergue* "sus-

---

[32] For a detailed eyewitness account of the revolution see Blair Thomson, *Ethiopia: The Country That Cut Off Its Head* (London: Robson Books, 1975).
[33] Peter Koehn, "Ethiopian Politics: Military Intervention and Prospects for Further Change," *Africa Today*, vol. 22 (April-June 1975), p. 10.
[34] Ibid., p. 11.

pended Parliament and the Constitution, dissolved the Crown Council and the Imperial Court, disbanded the Emperor's personal military staff, nationalized his palace, and arrested Haile Selassie."[35] It formally assumed power on September 12, 1974, with General Aman Andom as chairman of the Provisional Military Administrative Council.

General Aman served as chairman for only a couple of months. Violence erupted in the form of a consolidating coup on November 22. Radical elements within the *Dergue* opposed General Aman's proposed mediation and political settlement with the Eritrean Liberation Front. General Aman was killed and sixty imprisoned aristocrats, former government officials, and military figures were executed for crimes against the Ethiopian people.[36] With their position solidified, the *Dergue* appointed Brigadier General Teferi Benti as their figurehead chairman, but real power appeared to rest in the hands of Major Mengistu Haile Mariam, Benti's vice chairman, and Major Atenafu Abate, described as a dogmatic Marxist, second vice chairman.[37]

When the *Dergue* formally took control in September, they adopted the motto *"Ethiopia Tikdem,"* meaning "Ethiopia First." The significance of this motto became clear on December 13 when the *Dergue* virtually declared Ethiopia to be a Socialist state.[38] The administrative, economic, and social programs instituted by the *Dergue* since December 1974 reflect the fundamental principles of Ethiopian socialism summarized as "equality, self-reliance, the dignity of labor, the supremacy of the common good, and the indivisibility of Ethiopian unity."[39] However, change does not come quickly and the problems of Eritrea, land and tax reforms, labor and student unrest, and a dismal economy continue to plague the country. On March 21, 1975, the monarchy was formally abolished by proclamation, and later that year, on August 27, former Emperor Haile Selassie died in detention.

Organizational Factors

The political role of the military in a state is shaped largely by the interaction of organizational and environmental factors peculiar to that state. With the historical perspective established, we turn now

---

[35] Ibid., p. 12.
[36] Thomson, *Ethiopia*, p. 120.
[37] Ibid., p. 132.
[38] Ibid., p. 131.
[39] "Ethiopia," in *1976 Britannica Book of the Year* (Chicago: Encyclopaedia Britannica, 1976), p. 335.

to a description and discussion of the organization and characteristics of the armed forces in Ethiopia. Their interaction with environmental factors will be discussed later.

The Ethiopian Armed Forces. Ethiopia's military forces are ideally structured for their conventional missions of preserving the country's territorial integrity and supplementing the police in internal security activities. With a total armed force of about 44,800 in mid-1975, they were fully capable of fulfilling these tasks. Additional sources of emergency reinforcement included the 8,000-man, provincially based Territorial Army, a mobile emergency police force of 6,800, a 3,200-man commando force, and about 1,200 frontier guards.[40]

The army, known officially as the Ethiopian Ground Force, made up over 90 percent of the total military force in 1975 and placed primary emphasis on infantry. The elite Imperial Bodyguard, which was more fully integrated into the regular army structure after the unsuccessful coup attempt of 1960, was the most professional and modern military unit during Haile Selassie's reign. The 2,300-man Imperial Ethiopian Air Force was trained and structured to accomplish air defense, close air support, and ground attack missions. The small Imperial Ethiopian Navy, about 1,500 men with a total of fifteen ships, operated as a coast guard unit within the territorial waters off Eritrea Province.

It is not known what changes if any the Provisional Military Administrative Council has made in the organization of the Ethiopian armed forces. Under Haile Selassie, the organizational structure of the military establishment was very much like that found in the United States. The emperor, by constitutional provision, was commander in chief of the armed forces and exercised supreme authority. The minister of national defense was the cabinet officer exercising regular administrative supervision of the armed forces. The Office of the Chief of Staff of the Imperial Ethiopian Armed Forces formed the headquarters and control center of the three component services, and its joint staff performed the usual administrative functions.

The armed forces under Haile Selassie enjoyed little autonomy in major decisions. In addition to the assumption of direct command in time of war, the emperor reserved the right to determine the size, organization, and command structure of the forces together with the power to appoint, promote, transfer, and dismiss military officers. The responsibilities that remained within the emperor's province

---

[40] "The Military Balance 1975/76," The International Institute for Strategic Studies, London, England, in *Air Force Magazine*, December 1975, pp. 74-75.

were nonexclusive, but they included appeals in courts-martial, awards and decorations, changes in strength and equipment, the military budget, major strategic plans, and the acquisition and construction of major military facilities.[41] Authority for final action on military matters not reserved to the emperor was vested in the minister of national defense. With such supreme authority, Haile Selassie was able to exercise, at least until mid-1974, effective personal control over the military.

Recruitment in the armed forces is voluntary for both enlisted men and officers, and Ethiopia has had no trouble satisfying its manning requirements with less than 1 percent of the potential military manpower available on active duty in the late 1960s.[42] Enlisted personnel are recruited primarily from the rural youth and the unemployed in the cities and most have very little education. In ethnic composition, the enlisted force is primarily Amhara, though it includes some Tigreans and a heavy admixture of Galla.[43] The officer corps has evolved as an educated and professional elite with heavy recruitment from secondary school seniors and first-year college students. Its ethnic distribution is not precisely known, but considering the three major ethnic groups, it appears that over 50 percent of the officers are Amhara, around 25 percent are Tigrean, and approximately 10 percent are Galla.[44] Most come from upper- and middle-class families.

Haile Selassie recognized early in his career the importance of education and training in building a modern and professional military force. By the time the Italians had invaded in 1935, he had sent some officers to France to study at the Saint Cyr Military Academy, brought a military mission from Belgium to train his Imperial Bodyguard, and established the Holeta Military Academy under Swedish management. Holeta was restored after the Italian occupation and later became the army's Infantry School. Today each service has its own academy: the Imperial Naval College at Massawa, Haile Selassie Military Academy at Harrar, and Haile Selassie I Air Force Academy at Debre Zeyt. In addition to strictly military and technical courses, these schools teach a variety of academic and practical subjects. Their general educational objectives include the subordination of ethnic loyalty to national loyalty, the substitution of professional competence and discipline for the traditional military ethic of martial

---

[41] Kaplan, *Area Handbook*, p. 485.
[42] Ibid., p. 488.
[43] Levine, "Military in Ethiopian Politics," p. 15.
[44] Ibid., p. 15.

enthusiasm and wanton bravery, and the replacement of political ambition through military service with an ethic of professional duty to country.[45]

Characteristics of the Military in Ethiopia. Although the military organization within a state can be adequately described under the headings mission, structure, typology, autonomy, recruitment, and education, other characteristics must be considered in an evaluation of the propensity of the military for involvement in the political realm. The more important characteristics in this regard are the degree of political awareness, the values held by the military, the level of cohesion existing within the armed forces, and the nature and extent of military professionalism.

A high degree of political awareness was deeply ingrained in the historical development of the Ethiopian military culture. Haile Selassie's attempts during the 1940s to differentiate between the civilian and military realms by depriving provincial lords of their private armies and by assigning civilian functions to civilians and military functions to professional soldiers primarily served to strengthen his personal authority and control rather than to decrease the political awareness of the military. After the army suppressed the coup attempted by the Imperial Bodyguard in 1960, a new political consciousness began to emerge in the Ethiopian military. This consciousness was reinforced in later years by the contacts the military had abroad and by the recognition that it shared important concerns with students and the young educated elite.

It has been suggested that the primary values espoused by most of the Ethiopian military are national independence, technical modernization, and social welfare.[46] Although most military men are not interested in territorial expansion, there appears to be strong feeling within the present military government that Eritrea must remain an integral part of Ethiopia. Their concerns for more rapid modernization and social welfare were visible during the "Creeping Coup" in 1974.

A high level of cohesion has never been characteristic of the Ethiopian military. The absence of cohesion has been an outgrowth of the traditional military culture and the personal ability of Haile Selassie to check, balance, and divide the armed forces internally while building a modern professional force. Prior to the 1974 coup, tensions within the military appeared to be caused by differences between the

---
[45] Ibid.
[46] Ibid., p. 22.

conservative, traditional group of older officers and the radical, progressive younger cadres. Conflict and cleavages within the ruling military committee were readily apparent in the conduct of the coup itself when General Aman was killed and many imprisoned officials and military figures executed.

As in many developing countries, in Ethiopia the military has evolved as the most professional and technologically proficient institution. While taking action to curb the powers of the traditional elites and centralize power in his person, Haile Selassie gradually built a modern and professional military force. Professionalism and technological proficiency in the political and economic sectors of Ethiopian society, regardless of increased emphasis on education, have not kept pace with progress in the military.

Environmental Factors

The nature of the military as a national institution is formed by the environment in which it develops. A discussion of the political, economic, and social framework and institutions, the legitimacy enjoyed by the government, and the existence or absence of internal and external threats will serve to describe those environmental factors most pertinent to the investigation of civil-military relations in Ethiopia.

Framework and Institutions. Until the 1974 coup, Ethiopia was a centralized unitary monarchy with absolute power vested in the emperor by constitutional authority. The supreme personal authority exercised by Haile Selassie permeated the entire structure of government. While ministers were responsible for daily operations within their respective areas, major decisions were the exclusive realm of the emperor. Parliament existed primarily as a deliberative body, since legislation with any chance for final enactment had to come from the emperor. The Crown Council served as the emperor's advisory body to review legislation being submitted to the Parliament. Haile Selassie created a bureaucratic, highly fragmented form of central government, which was inefficient, ineffective, and highly susceptible to manipulation and control by the skillful emperor.

Government administration below the national level extends to 14 provinces, 99 subprovinces, about 440 districts, and roughly 1,330 subdistricts.[47] Governors and major officials at the provincial level

---

[47] Markakis, *Ethiopia: Traditional Polity*, p. 290.

and below were either appointed by the emperor himself or appointed subject to his approval. At the base of provincial administration is the village headman, whose position involves all the responsibilities of the village chief in a traditional peasant society. As would be expected, the influence and control of the emperor and the central government decreased at the lower echelons of administration—and decreased with increasing distance from the capital at Addis Ababa.

Ethiopia has now abolished the title of kingdom but has not officially been declared a republic. Loosely, it could be termed a Socialist state headed by a military junta. The 1974 coup has apparently not disrupted to any great extent the organization and administration of government below the national level.

Regardless of the provisions of the Revised Constitution of 1955, strong political institutions other than the monarchy were never allowed to develop under Haile Selassie. The dispersion of power among monarchy, church, and nobility existing around 1900, which gradually changed to a concentration of power in Haile Selassie, has been adequately documented. Political parties, an important factor in the political and economic development of many modernizing states, have never existed in Ethiopia. Their absence has been explained by the role of the emperor and a "lack of those historical factors that elsewhere stimulated the development of African political parties."[48]

The economic framework in Ethiopia rests on a feudal system of subsistence agriculture with a relatively minor but growing contribution from manufacturing. The problems associated with the multitude of different and complex land tenure systems have plagued the Ethiopian government for years. Land reform is badly needed, for Ethiopia has great agricultural potential. However, traditional forces have consistently resisted attempts at land reform, and the system today remains relatively unchanged. The significance of major land reform is reflected in one authority's opinion that it "would create a political vacuum and undermine the country's political and social structure."[49] If the *Dergue* can enforce the land reform measures instituted in 1975, a gradual improvement in the Ethiopian economy may take place.

Because Ethiopia is so dependent on subsistence agriculture, unfavorable climatic conditions can cause major problems. The absence

---

[48] Robert L. Hess with Gerhard Loewenberg, "The Ethiopian No-Party State," *American Political Science Review*, vol. 58 (1964), p. 947.

[49] Barbara A. Alpert, "The Ethiopian Perplex," *Current History*, vol. 60 (March 1971), p. 154.

of normally heavy rains in the highlands in 1972 led to drought and famine conditions beginning in 1973 and extending to the present. The government's poor handling of these conditions was one of the causes of the 1974 coup d'état.

Resource allocation is another factor that has affected the economic environment in Ethiopia. Although the budget was prepared by the Council of Ministers, Haile Selassie maintained strict control over the budgetary process, acting as final arbiter in the case of disputes. Defense has consistently been the largest single item in the budget, varying from 19 percent to 24 percent of annual appropriations throughout the 1960s and averaging about 2.4 percent of the gross national product in the late 1960s.[50]

In general, Ethiopian society can be described as predominantly rural, consisting of many diverse peoples, tribes, and ethnic groups. Probably less than 10 percent of the population live in or near the relatively few urban centers; in these areas, the military is closely integrated with society. The civilian attitude toward the military is ambivalent. While the armed forces are appreciated for defending the nation's territorial integrity and admired for the traditional virtues and style of life connected with masculine virility, they are also mistrusted and regarded as parasitic.[51]

The character of the traditional social system in Ethiopia is such that individual rather than collective ambition is encouraged. As Donald N. Levine wrote: "There are no fixed corporate structures, either in the kinship system or on a territorial or civic basis, which might channel the pursuit of common interests."[52] This characteristic, which served to support Haile Selassie's personal authority, will continue to work to the advantage of the military regime by preventing the formation of contending sources of control.

Legitimacy. Until 1974, the legitimacy of imperial rule rested on the emperor's personal ability, his support from the church, the nobility, and the military, and his claim to descent from the Solomonic Dynasty acknowledged in the Revised Constitution of 1955.[53] With the monarchy now officially abolished, the Provisional Military Administrative Council has moved to legitimize its own claim to rule through

---

[50] Kaplan, *Area Handbook*, p. 487.
[51] Levine, "Military in Ethiopian Politics," pp. 23-24.
[52] Ibid., p. 18.
[53] Christopher S. Clapham, "Imperial Leadership in Ethiopia," *African Affairs*, vol. 68 (April 1969), p. 111.

the use of force and the solicitation of support from the traditional institutions and the populace.

Legitimacy in government is enhanced by an established and accepted system for the orderly transfer of political power. Such a system has never existed in Ethiopia, even though the Revised Constitution of 1955 provided for lineal succession. In reality, succession has largely been determined throughout Ethiopian history by power politics.

A low level of political awareness and participation among the civilian population is not uncommon in the modernizing third world countries. One factor that helps to promote political awareness and participation is a high literacy rate, but Ethiopia has one of the lowest literacy rates in Africa. While the national literacy rate in 1969 was claimed to be around 10 percent, wide variations, from 56 percent in Addis Ababa to 3 percent in Wollo Province, existed within the country.[54] Political awareness, too, is highest in Ethiopia around the cities and among students, workers, civil servants, and the educated elite. The vast majority, the rural poor, are concerned only with the lower levels of government and the traditional landlord-tenant relationships. In addition, because lines of communication are poor, political awareness lessens with increasing distance from the seat of central government.

The Revised Constitution of 1955 provided for popular election of the Chamber of Deputies, and the first election in Ethiopian history was held in 1957. A review of registration and voting in the four elections held between 1957 and 1969 indicates an extremely low voter participation rate, in spite of a concerted effort by the government to stimulate public participation.[55]

Italy posed the only serious external threat to Ethiopia in the twentieth century, and the Italian occupation was the impetus for the building of a modern Ethiopian military. Of the neighboring countries, only Kenya has maintained cordial relations with Ethiopia. Border disputes with Somalia and Sudan in the 1960s required the use of the armed forces, but these conflicts were not important enough to have a unifying effect in the country as a whole. Although there have been many minor uprisings by various tribes and groups in the provinces, the greatest internal threat has been, and continues to be, the problem of Eritrea. Eritrea has had both unifying and divisive effects on the country and the military. Differences over how to handle the problem during the 1974 coup led to the emergence of

---

[54] Hess, *Ethiopia*, p. 157.
[55] Markakis, *Ethiopia: Traditional Polity*, pp. 278-81.

radical elements that were able to take control in the Provisional Military Administrative Council.

Summary

Two distinct phases in the pattern of military involvement in Ethiopian politics are apparent. The first phase was the product of historical processes beginning with the Kingdom of Aksum and ending with the Italian occupation between 1935 and 1941. Throughout this period, the military was fully integrated into the traditional political, economic, and social systems.

The second phase, more complex, evolved from the personal efforts of Haile Selassie to concentrate power in the monarchy at the expense of the Ethiopian Orthodox Church and the nobility, build a professional and modern military, and modernize his country. But modernization, according to Huntington, confronts the absolute monarch in a traditional political system with a basic dilemma: modernization requires centralized power and control; but successful modernization generates new institutions, increases political participation, and disperses power. Specifically, in the case of Ethiopia under Haile Selassie, Huntington says:

> On the one hand, centralization of power in the monarchy was necessary to promote social, cultural, and economic reform. On the other hand, this centralization made difficult or impossible the expansion of the power of the traditional polity and the assimilation into it of the new groups produced by modernization. The participation of these groups in politics seemingly could come only at the price of the monarchy.[56]

Haile Selassie paid that price in 1974.

There were numerous instances of militant opposition during Haile Selassie's reign, but few involved the military itself as an antagonist. Aristocratic conspiracies were usually discovered early and easily dispelled. Peasant revolts were more troublesome. Although these were usually suppressed by the provincial police and the Territorial Army, some required the use of the national armed forces. The Eritrean rebellion has been the most serious and significant internal threat to the central authority under Haile Selassie and the *Dergue*.

---

[56] Samuel P. Huntington, *Political Order in Changing Societies* (New Haven: Yale University Press, 1968), p. 177.

In the face of all of these threats, the military remained loyal to the emperor. Significant internal military involvement with the opposition came only with the unsuccessful coup in 1960 and the successful coup in 1974.

Military support for the emperor started to decline after the coup attempt in 1960 by the Imperial Bodyguard. Although the coup was instigated by an element of the military, it did not gain the support of the armed forces as a whole. Traditional loyalty to the authority of the emperor, low internal cohesion within the military, and a low level of political awareness among the majority of the armed forces were major factors in the failure of the coup. The dissatisfaction expressed by the coup leaders and their civilian advocates with the rate of modernization supports Huntington's proposition.

In the period from 1960 to 1974, the political consciousness of the military grew; new institutions, such as labor organizations, began to form, and existing social and political forces, such as students and young bureaucrats, gathered strength—while imperial power and authority gradually eroded. The military demanded and received several pay increases and other concessions from the emperor. Labor organizations conducted strikes and demonstrations over the issues of inflation and government corruption. Students expressed their dissatisfaction with government policies and the rate of modernizing reform through agitation and unrest. All in all, the political and social climate had become one in which a clash between the forces favoring rapid reform and the forces of traditional imperial authority was inevitable.

In 1974 the opportunity and disposition for active military intervention were decidedly present. The immediate causes of intervention were testimony to the declining legitimacy of Haile Selassie's government. The coup started slowly in early 1974 with a natural unfolding of events in a charged political, economic, and social environment. While no single organized element within either the military or society can be seen to have instigated the coup, it appears that events were set in motion by mutinies within the armed forces. The rebellion gathered momentum and the military, the most disciplined, professional, and technologically proficient institution, emerged to take control. As demands were made and concessions granted, dissidents in the military became more aware of their political power and of the relative weakness of the traditional forces. Cohesiveness within the military was lacking, and it took almost nine months and a coup-within-a-coup to overcome internal divisions within the Provisional Military Administrative Council. The executions in November 1974 reduced the possibility of a counter-coup by conservative and traditional forces.

During the first year of military government, the *Dergue* announced the format for political, social, and economic reform through a series of proclamations. Its success will depend in large measure on the support it receives from competing civilian institutions and the population. It should be noted, however, that the *Dergue* now faces a dilemma very much like that which Huntington described as confronting Haile Selassie.

What will be the pattern of civil-military relations in Ethiopia in the future? Though the *Dergue* professes the intention of returning government eventually to civilian hands, experience in other praetorian states suggests that government will probably remain with the military for some time. There seems to be no civilian institution strong enough to challenge the military for control. There is also a real possibility, considering the lack of cohesion within the junta, that internal conflict could weaken the power of the *Dergue* and generate a military counter-coup. Whether or not this will happen only time can tell.

4

REMARKS ON "EDUCATIONAL ASPECTS OF CIVIL-MILITARY RELATIONS"

Orville D. Menard

Public Opinion and the Military

"The remedy for the vices of the army is not to be found in the army itself, but in the country," Alexis de Tocqueville pointedly observed.[1] His comment reminds us that a nation and its military are not separate and distinct entities, but that the military's role in society, its mission and self-perceptions, are consequences of surrounding environmental factors. Too often the issue of civil-military relations is addressed in terms of the military, with scant attention to the civilian side of the equation. But the political attitudes and actions of any army or any armed service can be understood only if we understand the political attitudes and actions of the civilian community.

"An army is an emanation of the nation it serves," I wrote some years ago,

> reflecting social, political, and technological foundations. To study an army is to gain insights into the nation it serves because a nation and its army are interdependent. An army is not a mirror image of the nation, nor a microcosm—the nation writ small; it is, in organization, purposes, attitudes, and behavior, conditioned by the sustaining state.[2]

As a result, force levels, strategies, and weaponry become those sanctioned by the civilian political leadership and the people they lead. For a number of years—the cold war years—America's leaders and people shared a view of the international environment and our nation's

---

[1] Alexis de Tocqueville, *Democracy in America*, 2 vols. (Boston: John Allyn, 1873), vol. 2, p. 331.
[2] Orville D. Menard, *The Army and the Fifth Republic* (Lincoln: University of Nebraska Press, 1967), pp. 5-6.

responsibilities: our object, they agreed, was to contain communism. Today we are divided in our interpretations of the international political scene and also in our appreciation of the roles and obligations of our national institutions. We assented to presidential dominance in the national security field throughout the 1940s, 1950s, and 1960s. Currently Congress, or at least part of it, is attempting to reassert its voice in defense and foreign policy. Its efforts are greeted with sighs of "at last" from a number of us, with chagrin from others who harbor reservations concerning the legislative branch's constitutional responsibilities and capabilities in foreign affairs.

General Goodpaster's paper is representative of a school of thought that regards U.S. (or free world) relations with the U.S.S.R. and China (Communist world) as basically hostile. "So long as the outward reach for domination over others by Communist regimes under the direction of Moscow and Peking continues," Goodpaster warns, "our interests may be endangered at many points." America's world responsibilities, he says, include protecting Western Europe, preventing foreign military intervention in Latin America, giving support and reassurance to other areas, such as Australia, New Zealand, "key areas" of the Middle East, and Indonesia and the Philippines, and

> giving support, when so directed, to the independence and sovereignty of free nations of the world threatened from outside; maintaining the capability of intervention in areas of the world that our highest political authority may deem sufficiently critical to the security interests of the United States to justify such intervention in time of crisis.

Few would disagree that this is a "full and demanding agenda for our security authorities and for their supporting staffs."

Goodpaster's paper also reveals a certain skepticism toward recent foreign policy decisions of the U.S. Congress. Congress's position on such foreign policy matters as Vietnam and Angola Goodpaster perceives as demonstrating an unwillingness to make or support American commitments and an equal unwillingness to indicate what U.S. commitments Congress will support. A question posed in the Library of Congress study of the U.S.-Soviet military balance released on February 11, 1976, may be of interest here: "What commitments contribute least to U.S. security?"[3]

---

[3] U.S. Congress, Senate, Committee on Armed Forces, *United States/Soviet Military Balance*, by John M. Collins and John S. Chwat, Library of Congress Congressional Research Service, Committee Print (Washington, D.C.: U.S. Government Printing Office, 1976), p. 36.

The implications of the U.S.S.R./China threat, as Goodpaster perceives it, in terms of military preparedness and capabilities are clear, as are the attendant consequences for allocation of our resources. However, as Goodpaster comments, there is no consensus in the United States today. The considered judgment of some that the Soviet Union and China remain bent upon expansion, territorial and ideological, is challenged by the considered judgment of others that we have entered an international era in which our purpose and will, and those of others, must be reexamined. It is an era in which a posture of worldwide military preparedness may be beyond our capabilities or, indeed, unnecessary, and which fails to recognize the limits of both our own power and that of the Soviet Union and China.

Advocates of this latter school of thought are led to different conceptions of necessary force levels, equipment needs, and international responsibilities from those based on the view that tensions and threats still underlie an ongoing worldwide mission for the United States. The debate in Congress over the 1977 fiscal year defense budget afforded interesting examples of foreign policy perceptions and their effects on national security spending. Moreover, our lack of consensus extends to attitudes toward Congress. Certainly there are critics of Congress who are especially doubtful about its role as a foreign policy decision maker. But there also are those who welcome its resurgence, the decline of the "imperial presidency," and legislation such as the War Powers Act. They regard the strictures imposed by Congress in relation to Vietnam and Angola as foreign policy initiatives, long overdue, that signal the restoration of the constitutional balance between the executive and legislative branches.

It is not our purpose here to decide which view is the more true and the more accurate, but merely to discuss the connection between opinion and the role of the armed forces. When the international environment was widely perceived as hostile, the result was the public's willingness to support a large military establishment and the strategies to guide it; military men found their roles in society and in government harmonious and accepted to an extent seldom encountered in our peacetime history. However, with the aftermath of Vietnam and the new disagreement over the present and future nature of world politics, the domestic environment has altered and the military's proper status in American life once more is a matter of debate. Distrust, misgivings, and resentments toward the military, attitudes that we associate with pre-World War II America, have been reborn. As General Goodpaster notes, "the mood is unquestionably disinterested, negative, even hostile, though in some quarters the intensity of feelings seems to be lessening."

The Dangers of an Alienated Army

General Goodpaster speculates as to whether this "alienation" will persist—alienation, as he sees it, between the military and "others concerned with national security" on one side, and the media and the "academic community in particular" on the other. In passing, I would suggest that "others concerned with national security" can be found on both sides of the issue and that many individuals in the media and the academy are concerned with national security.

It is the word alienation that attracts our attention, along with the immediate concerns it evokes in the context of our symposium topic, the educational aspects of civil-military relations. Recall the events that brought Charles de Gaulle back to power: the French army, long bound by a tradition of civilian control of the military and nicknamed the "Great Mute" because of its lack of a political voice, bluntly entered French political life in May 1958 and de Gaulle, the army's choice, assumed national leadership. When it became clear that de Gaulle was not going to maintain Algeria as part of France, which was the army's fundamental political goal, elements of the army perpetrated a *Putsch* in April 1961. Though it had been successful three years earlier in bringing de Gaulle to power, the army failed in its attempt to oust him. Students of France and civil-military relations searched for explanations as to why the apolitical French army had become an active political force. Their answer: the French army had become an alienated army. It had come to feel betrayed by the politicians of the Palais Bourbon, humiliated by defeats it blamed on Paris, and abandoned by the civilians, and it lamented its members' being reduced to what they considered second-class status as citizens. Certainly the word alienation is one to attract the notice of students of civil-military relations.[4]

Through the study of military involvement in politics, many factors and influences are discovered that help explain the very common phenomenon of political armies. But Samuel Finer, as a result of his civil-military investigations, posits two basic considerations as starting points for analysis: the first is the disposition of an army to intervene in politics, the second, the opportunity to intervene. When

---

[4] See ibid. and John S. Ambler, *The French Army in Politics* (Columbus: Ohio State University Press, 1966), and George A. Kelly, *Lost Soldiers* (Cambridge: The M.I.T. Press, 1965).

these coincide the military becomes a dominant political force. The disposition to intervene issues from frustrations, from alienation, that leaves an army ill disposed to take orders from the civilians and inclined to issue them itself. According to Finer, the matter of opportunity is related to the strength of civilian institutions, that is, the degree to which the civilian population is attached to its form of government and is willing to support it.[5]

In 1958 France had an alienated army and a civilian population that had lost its faith in the Fourth Republic. A politically disposed army plus a politically disaffected citizenry brought an end to their government. On the other hand, when in 1961 elements of the French army, now alienated from de Gaulle's France, attempted to overthrow him, the civilians supported the government, and the *Putsch* failed. Disposition was present but not opportunity.

The United States has a long and strong tradition of civilian control of the military—but so did France, and so did Portugal and Ethiopia and Chile. We cannot assume civilian control to be an unalterable state of affairs, but rather something we must strive to preserve. An alienated army is a politically dangerous army. When it is combined with widespread disillusionment with civil institutions and distrust of politics and politicians, the scenario for military intervention is complete.

Our armed forces are not alienated in the profound sense that the French army was, and their acceptance of civilian control is still firmly embedded in the military code of behavior. One survey of articles published in military and military-related periodicals between 1968 and 1972 (years when the frustrations faced by the U.S. military must have been great) concluded that there was then "no clarion call for a disavowal of the traditional military professional ethics of civil-military relations within the United States Government." [6]

Even during the months and years when Watergate was jarring the nation, there was no fear of the military's deposing Nixon and assuming power. With slight opportunity and little disposition, the military offers no challenge to civilian control. However, should the disposition develop and should an opportunity appear, we would be as susceptible to overt military political involvement as other nations have been when these factors have come into consonance. Avoiding

---

[5] Samuel E. Finer, *The Man on Horseback* (New York: Frederick A. Praeger, 1962), chapters 4, 5, 6.
[6] John R. Probert, "Vietnam and the United States Military Thought Concerning Civil-Military Roles in Government," in Charles L. Cochran, ed., *Civil-Military Relations* (New York: The Free Press, 1974), p. 151.

such an eventuality is the essence of maintaining civilian control of the military. It follows that we must counter moves toward alienation among our armed forces and sustain civilian attachment to and support for civil institutions. Not that the institutions cannot or should not change; the essential word here is *attachment*, not *institutions*, for the latter may change but must retain their civilian essence.

The Role of Education

General Goodpaster states the need for educating the military in the substance of civil-military relations. We must similarly educate civilians. In the former instance, efforts should be directed toward maintaining what I call an integrated army. By that I mean an army that shares our nation's basic social and political values, an army not separate from the nation but an integral part of it. Surely the functional and professional requirements of the military profession suggest that the armed forces will remain in certain ways distinct. But distinct does not mean separate or autonomous. It is used here in the sense of identifiably different. In values, aspirations, and understanding the armed forces must remain a part of the whole society.

General Goodpaster's paper indicates the educational efforts of the services to this end. The survey referred to above also reveals the military's eagerness to acquire officers better educated in national and international politics.

The U.S. military has engaged in a great deal of introspection since Vietnam, as every army is wont to do after unsatisfactory engagements. Self-criticism and self-evaluation have characterized our officer corps in recent years, an example that could well be followed by other elements of our society including the academic community, whose general posture is one of self-satisfaction. Academicians should examine the educational aspects of civil-military relations with a view to educating our nonmilitary citizens in the substance of civil-military relations, just as Goodpaster recommends that our military citizens be educated.

Civilian control in the United States is most often taken as a given, an element of tradition enshrined in the Constitution, ensuring that a *Seven Days in May* scenario will never be realized. But civilian control of the military is not a natural state for a polity and may even be unnatural considering the experiences of others. Education, as one of many other environmental factors, provides a means to promote the integrated civil-military relationship our nation desires, and as such it should be directed at the civilian as well as the military sector.

Educators have the responsibility to expose their students to the interrelated condition of soldier and state, to remind them that armies are emanations of the nation and people that sustain them, to inform them of the military's legitimate pressure-group role in the political process, but also to warn them of the dangers that arise when the military or any of its branches crosses the border from legitimate expert advice to expert supervision couched in terms of national security.

Harold Lasswell, long ago in his famous Garrison State construct, postulated the threat to civilian control that exists in a world characterized by international tension, a threat typified not only by increased reliance on the specialists in violence, but also by an ever enhanced militarization of the civilian sector.[7] Militaristic citizens in the public at large, in Congress, and in the inner circles of the White House are reminders of Lasswell's warning. The universities should be mentioned again in this context, considering the importance of the defense-related contracts once so popular on our major campuses.

Thus, one task of education in civil-military relations, in relation to the general society within which both military and academy exist, is to promote the civil values and traditions of our nation. This does not mean dogged acceptance of the status quo, but the acceptance of political and other change, however unsettling, without a loss of faith in the civil nature of our polity.

In one of the most quoted speeches of modern times, a former professional soldier leaving the American presidency warned against the acquisition of unwarranted influence by the military-industrial complex. In a less frequently quoted portion of the speech, Dwight David Eisenhower affirmed the educational aspects of civil-military relations: "Only an alert and knowledgeable citizenry can compel the proper meshing of the huge industrial and military machinery of defense with our peaceful methods and goals, so that security and liberty may prosper together."[8]

Manifest in General Goodpaster's contribution to our symposium is the need for civil-military mutual understanding and harmony. The lack of mutuality and appreciation for the military's essential role

---

[7] Harold Lasswell, "The Garrison State and Specialists on Violence," *American Journal of Sociology*, vol. 46 (January 1941), pp. 455-68; see also Harold Lasswell, "The Garrison State Hypothesis Today," in Samuel P. Huntington, ed., *Changing Patterns of Military Politics* (New York: The Free Press of Glencoe, Inc., 1962), pp. 51-70.

[8] *New York Times*, January 18, 1961.

frequently sensed by members of our armed forces is captured in an anonymous verse inscribed on the grave of an English soldier:

> God and the soldier all men adore
> In time of war and nevermore.
> In time of peace when all is righted
> God is forgotten and the soldier slighted.

On the other hand, the guardian's attitude toward the guarded is revealed in the story about the young veteran who asked his Oxford tutor what *he* had done during the war. "Young man," was the reply, "I am the civilization you fought to preserve."